A Fool

for a

Client

My Struggle Against the Power
of a Public Prosecutor

by *Roy Cohn*

HAWTHORN BOOKS, INC.
Publishers
New York

In appreciation to my lawyers:
　　Frank G. Raichle—first trial
　　Joseph E. Brill—second trial
　　Tom Bolan and Dan Driscoll—all the way

PREFACE

ON DECEMBER 9, 1969, at the age of forty-two and with a great future behind me, I stood before a federal-court jury of eight men and four women in New York City. If convicted on the five-count criminal indictment, I faced a maximum forty-five years' imprisonment.

Summing up my own case, I said: "This is the first time in my life I have ever addressed a jury in behalf of a defendant in a criminal case. When I went to law school, little did I dream that my first time in this role would be in my own behalf."

The jurors had heard over two months of testimony, but it took them less than four hours to render a verdict. They filed into the courtroom shortly before 11 P.M. The ticks of the courtroom clock sounded like gunshots to me as the jury waited until the judge appeared.

The clerk asked if they had reached a verdict.

The foreman rose and said, "We have." I looked straight at him as he glanced down at a verdict sheet the judge had sent into the jury room. He announced the verdict on each of the counts: "Not guilty."

After the unanimous verdict the New York *Post* learned the basis for acquittal from some of the jurors. They said the verdict had been easy to reach—the Government's case wasn't believable. Asked which of the "Government" witnesses they believed, one juror told the newsmen, "None of them."

It was the second time I had been acquitted on each and every charge brought against me by an old political enemy, Robert Morgenthau, then United States Attorney for the Southern District of New York.

On July 16, 1964, on a bright summer morning, another federal-court jury had filed into that same courtroom. The clerk asked if they had reached a verdict on a nine-count criminal indictment against me; their unanimous verdict was "Not guilty." Again, in subsequent interviews, the jurors said they had not believed the prosecution witnesses.

So I had the opportunity for a future once again. Twice, American juries had unanimously acquitted me. And I was moved to say, "God bless America!"

But the question remains: When not one of twenty-four jurors in two trials accepted the United States Attorney's case, why and how did the cases come about? The answers point up some important problems in the administration of justice in America.

R. C.

CONTENTS

A Fool

for a Client

*My Struggle Against the Power
of a Public Prosecutor*

I

Why Me?

"IF I HAVE done anything good in my life, I expect no credit for it in this case. Nor do I expect to be blamed here for any past position I've taken with which you might not agree."

I spoke these words to the federal-court jury on December 9, 1969, shortly after I started the summation of a criminal case in which I myself was the defendant. Of course, I was aware of the possibility that my jurors had formed a general opinion of me back in the 1950's. The fact of my controversiality exists and always will. If I should die at one hundred years of age, my obituary will still read:

ROY COHN DEAD; WAS McCARTHY INVESTIGATIONS AIDE

NEW YORK. January 6, 2027, 11 A.M. Roy Cohn, former aide to Senator Joseph McCarthy, the notorious Communist witch-hunter of the 1950's, died at his residence a few minutes ago. Mr. Cohn had been an explorer and writer since he retired from law practice in 1998. Edward R. Murrow, who was a commentator on television, a system in wide use last century before the advent of totalvision, described Mr. Cohn

1

as an active practitioner of McCarthyism. McCarthyism denotes reckless, unsubstantiated accusation designed to destroy the reputations of innocent people.

The first step toward my present situation occurred after I was graduated from Columbia Law School at an age too young to take the bar examination. I had become impatient during my junior year in high school and had obtained permission from my father and from the headmaster of Horace Mann School for Boys to accelerate my education. I completed my senior-year courses over the summer and in the winter entered Columbia College. I made a sort of whirlwind tour through the college and through Columbia Law School, getting both degrees in under three and a half years. This was not due to any remarkable academic acumen on my part. It resulted rather from the fact that I attended summer sessions, and just after World War II, one could combine the first year of professional school with the last year of college.

I had spent summers working as a clerk for law firms, and I thought of doing so again while I waited to take the bar exam. But a wise and devoted friend, Appellate Division Justice Martin M. Frank, strongly urged that apprenticeship in the United States Attorney's office would be good training. The federal prosecutor was John F. X. McGohey, later a distinguished member of the federal bench. "You don't know anything, and you're not even old enough to be a lawyer," he greeted me when my interview for a job got under way. (I thought back on this when President Kennedy interviewed his brother Bobby for a slightly different post—Attorney General of the United States—and remarked, "Well, he has to learn how to practice law someplace.") Mr. McGohey hired me as a combination Photostat operator and law clerk. The day I was admitted to the bar the following year, I became an assistant United States Attorney.

Cases were assigned to the more experienced members of

the prosecutor's staff, but there was an office tradition that an assistant who had weekend duty would keep any case that broke while he was on standby. One Saturday morning a racketeer picked up a paper bag in front of a movie theater in the Bronx and drove it to the home of an evangelist in Harrison, New York. An arrest was made, and the paper bag was found to contain ten thousand dollars in counterfeit money. I was on weekend duty and drew the case. On that quiet Saturday morning of a slow news day an AP reporter trying to dig up a story casually asked me if we were closing in on a nationwide counterfeiting ring. I had never before dealt with the press, and I replied offhandedly that I supposed so —the bills had to have come from someplace. My shock when the afternoon papers headlined the nationwide crackdown news was matched by my chagrin on Monday morning when all my superiors from Mr. McGohey on down sent for me. Fortunately, I won the case, and it did lead to a nationwide counterfeiting ring.

My interest in internal-security cases began at a lunch in a New York restaurant with two FBI agents. We were there to discuss a case involving interstate transportation of counterfeit American Express checks, but we got on the subject of Alger Hiss. The lunch lasted for hours, and at its end some of my college-acquired beliefs about witch-hunts and red herrings were quite shaken. I was shocked at the documented story of Communist espionage and infiltration into government.

Thus began my specialization. I was a prosecutor of the second-string Communist leaders, the Remington perjury case, and of Julius and Ethel Rosenberg, convicted of atom spying. The Rosenberg case resulted in my first exposure to bitter controversy. The case itself was dramatic and important but uncomplicated. The Rosenbergs were deeply committed to communism. Mrs. Rosenberg recruited her younger brother, David Greenglass, to the cause. When in the service,

David was stationed in Los Alamos, New Mexico, and was assigned to a machine shop where models of sections of America's most closely guarded secret—the atomic bomb—were being constructed from plans drawn up by the top scientists who were assembled there.

The Rosenbergs persuaded Greenglass to turn sketches and information on the bomb over to them for transmission to the Kremlin. At the same time the Soviets had another friend who had penetrated the security blanket at Los Alamos. He was Dr. Klaus Fuchs, the head of the British Mission there and a Communist. Fuchs also turned over information on the bomb for transmission to Russia.

Harry Gold, a Communist courier, collected material from both Fuchs and Greenglass. When the FBI smashed the spy ring, Fuchs, then in England, was the first to be arrested. He told his story and identified the courier as Harry Gold, who was then arrested in the United States. The Rosenbergs knew, of course, that if Gold talked, the trial would lead to Greenglass and to them. They surreptitiously had passport pictures taken to prepare for an exit behind the Iron Curtain and urged Greenglass to do the same. But Greenglass wouldn't. Several other members of the ring did leave the country. Another one, Morton Sobell, got as far as Mexico, where he used false names and attempted to obtain passage to his Utopia, but before he could escape, he was discovered by the Mexican police and returned to the United States.

The trial was relatively short, and the prosecution's evidence was overwhelmingly strong. The jury unanimously convicted Sobell and the Rosenbergs, and the latter received the death sentence. After the trial, to some, the Rosenbergs became a *cause célèbre*. The Communist press even argued that imposing the death sentence was a result of anti-Semitism, though the prosecutors and the judge themselves were Jewish. Hundreds of thousands of dollars were raised by national committees studded with the usual bleeding-hearts. Of course, no such committees were organized for prison-camp or torture-chamber victims of Communist oppression.

The propaganda generated by the Rosenberg case has been intense and enduring. A recent manifestation was a short-lived Broadway production called *Inquest*. Though claiming to be historically accurate, I believe the play totally distorted the trial, omitting, for example, the facts that the Rosenbergs denied under oath having passport photos taken in an attempt to escape and that the Government then produced the photographer who took the photos. The play concludes with an impassioned attack on the judge and the system by the Rosenbergs' lawyer, the late Emanuel Bloch, when, in fact, after the trial was over and the verdict against his clients known, Bloch rose to say: "I believe that in this posture of the case, in retrospect, we can all say that we attempted to have this case tried as we expect criminal cases to be tried in this country; we tried to keep out extraneous issues; we tried to conduct ourselves as lawyers, and I know the Court conducted itself as an American judge."

The producers did not bring out the fact that the conviction was affirmed by the United States Court of Appeals and approved in an opinion by Judge Jerome Frank, one of the architects of the New Deal, and that the Supreme Court rejected seven appeals. The play's blatant bias was recognized by almost all the reviewers. Jack O'Brian wrote: "It should run for years—in Russia."

The 1970 production held some personal interest for me. I was portrayed on stage by a young Israeli actor named Michael Bursten. He had written me an amiable letter, and we made an appointment to meet. But he was ordered to cancel the appointment by the show's "higher-ups." I guess they wanted to avoid any accuracies that might creep into the show.

A year after the Rosenberg case, with the 1952 election of Eisenhower as President and the re-election of Joseph Mc-

Carthy as United States Senator, I went to Washington as chief counsel for the Senate Investigations Subcommittee. McCarthy was its chairman. During the two-year congressional session I was praised as a defender of America and freedom, as an opponent of communism, as a man who helped Senator McCarthy and the committee expose Red infiltration in government and industry. On the other hand, I was attacked for being a smear artist—one who trampled on civil rights and ruined people's reputations by false accusation.

It was this McCarthy period that for good or bad put its brand on me, and it is no doubt related to the legal difficulties I had in the 1960's.

When I asked myself why I had become the target of the Attorney General's dogged investigations, I could eliminate the possibility that he thought I ran the underworld or peddled drugs. I don't rob banks or kill or deliberately hurt people. I don't even smoke, and I drink too much only occasionally. I don't riot or throw stones in demonstrations.

I do admit to displaying a certain and perhaps inexcusable lack of tact. I recall walking into a meeting of a number of distinguished lawyers at the offices of a client of theirs and mine, an executive of a large corporation, who was facing a major litigation. The lawyers seemed stuffy and cautious to the point of being ineffective. I broke in with a suggestion, which our client accepted. Lou Nichols, who entered the business field after a quarter of a century at the side of J. Edgar Hoover in building the FBI, was at the meeting. He pulled me aside and gave me hell. I said, "But my idea was right." He replied, "Yes, it was. But the other lawyers have egos, too. You should have heard them out first. And when you made your point, you should have first complimented them on their ideas and made yours seem like a slight variation on theirs."

But when I entered government service at the age of twenty, I learned that one could respect seniority and the prevailing custom of keeping to a leisurely pace and accomplish nothing.

Or one could ignore the establishment, work hard, and get the job done. I followed the latter course and made enemies. And I imagine there are people with justifiable beefs about my actions. But none of these attitudes seems to be a criminally indictable offense.

Then why me? "The zeal with which the U.S. Attorney in New York has gone after Roy Cohn over a period of years suggests either that Mr. Cohn is soon to be revealed as head of S.M.E.R.S.H. or that the U.S. Attorney is suffering from a devil fixation," wrote William F. Buckley, Jr., in his column. Since I am not the head of S.M.E.R.S.H., we are left with two propositions. First, because of the hatred of McCarthy in many quarters and my association with "McCarthyism," someone who went after me would automatically attract wide support from the communications media and would presumably start with a large percentage of jurors potentially sympathetic to him and antagonistic to me. Secondly, someone would have to have a strong personal dislike for me to exploit the first factor. The Roberts Kennedy and Morgenthau fitted these conditions.

Bobby Kennedy and I had worked together for Senator Joe McCarthy some ten years before. Although we both had a close relationship with McCarthy, we never liked each other. I was chief counsel for the McCarthy Committee, a job Bobby had wanted, and he was assistant counsel. Because of the strain between us, he ran his show directly, as I did mine. Kennedy's principal investigation for McCarthy was of Greek shipowners transshipping goods to Iron Curtain countries. (Possibly, he reacted with distaste to his sister-in-law's future spouse.)

Then came the Army-McCarthy hearings, during which Bobby and I almost staged an unscheduled boxing match on television. Tempers were hot. When on the witness stand or acting as counsel for a witness, I faced the bank of senators grouped around the circular head table in the Senate caucus

room. Directly behind the Democrats, Bobby Kennedy was
peering out at me. My eyes would often meet his, and he
seemed visibly amused by the proceedings, particularly by my
testimony. Well, I wasn't. It was serious business for me.
While David Schine was being examined about some of his
suggestions to offset Soviet propaganda, Bobby gleefully fed
questions designed to ridicule us to the Democratic senators.
I was not in the mood for ridicule, and as we passed each
other on the way out of the hearing room, one word led to
another until I challenged him to settle matters outside. We
were kept apart, which was fortunate for me. My athletic
prowess was definitely secondary to his, and I would not have
been a good bet in that fight. We never had any direct contact thereafter.

Although he never admitted it, Morgenthau's hostility
toward me no doubt stems from my part in a senatorial
probe that involved his father, Henry Morgenthau, Jr. The
Soviet Union had made a bold attempt to get possession of
United States occupation-currency printing plates right after the end of World War II. If successful, it was to be the
first time in history that the United States had parted with
its currency plates. It would mean that hundreds of millions of dollars of American obligations could be printed
and used by the Communists without accountability to the
United States. Though a formidable task, it was not regarded as insurmountable by the Kremlin, which had already succeeded in stealing the atom-bomb sketches from
Los Alamos through Dr. Fuchs and David Greenglass. The
money-plate operation was approached by the Soviet Union
both officially and through the Communist underground in
the United States Treasury Department. The final word
would have to come from Secretary of the Treasury Henry
Morgenthau, Jr. His principal aide in the Treasury Department was Harry Dexter White, a Communist spy, whose
influence over Morgenthau was vast. The Soviet Union pre-

vailed. Over vigorous objections by Budget Director Daniel Bell, Morgenthau directed that the money plates be turned over.

In 1953 a Senate subcommittee chaired by Senator Karl Mundt, of South Dakota, investigated the matter. I served as counsel. The hearings developed the story, and the committee issued a report unanimously condemning Morgenthau's decision.

I don't believe I then knew that Secretary of the Treasury Morgenthau had a son named Robert, and I couldn't have been less interested. I had a job to do, and I did it. But Morgenthau did have a son named Robert, who became an intimate of the Kennedys. In 1960 he was working with the Kennedy team in Los Angeles. His reward for helping in the 1960 election campaign was his appointment the next year as United States Attorney for the Southern District of New York—with access to virtually unlimited funds and manpower and the right to subpoena books, records, and people for "investigation." After the election, when Kennedy became Attorney General of the United States, a former associate of Bobby Kennedy's and mine, as well as other mutual friends, tipped me off that Bobby was "out to get me." I hoped this wasn't true and that he would let bygones be bygones and go on to more important things. But I overlooked the reality that power often accentuates the desire to settle old scores.

I was subjected to an eighteen-month grand-jury investigation under Morgenthau's direction. As the grand jury's legal term was about to expire in September, 1963, a decision had to be made as to whether I should be criminally indicted. Despite the collapse of the theory on which the investigation had been predicated (a subject I will cover in later chapters), Morgenthau and Bobby Kennedy decided to go ahead with their plan to indict me. The decision was made at a meeting at Bobby's home in Virginia late one

September night. And when Bobby received the news of his brother's assassination, he was discussing my case at a luncheon with Morgenthau.

So as not to violate the Hatch Act, which prohibits political activity by federal officeholders, Robert Morgenthau had temporarily quit his post as United States Attorney in 1962 to be the Democratic nominee for governor of New York. His nomination was forced on the New York Democratic leadership headed by Congressman Charles A. Buckley, of the Bronx, who let his loyalty to the Kennedys outweigh his personal opinion of Morgenthau as a person and as a candidate. Buckley, a plain talker with an acerbic tongue, told me that Bobby Kennedy had telephoned him and asked him to support Morgenthau. Congressman Buckley replied: "Bobby, you picked a real stiff this time. The bum acts like he's sucking on a lemon all the time. But if you want him, I'll go along. But don't say I didn't warn you."

A pecular twist in the Morgenthau nomination boom was a Lou Harris poll, which showed Morgenthau, who wasn't well known, running very strong. This surprised most people. What would have surprised them even more was the fact that Morgenthau himself, when practicing law privately, had been one of the incorporators of the Harris poll when it was organized. So the poll that placed Morgenthau out front could have been called the Morgenthau poll. In any event the people spoke. Buckley was right, and Kennedy had picked a slow horse.

The idea that Morgenthau would resume his post as United States Attorney, which had been held open, immediately after losing the election, seemed to some not in keeping with the spirit of the Hatch Act, but Morgenthau was immediately reappointed and served until January, 1970. Apparently he had not recognized the results of the 1968 election and defied tradition by remaining on until 1970 to "finish his work." Not having personally prosecuted one case in eight years, there was a question as to what he was going to finish, and even *The New York Times* picked that argument apart by editorially commenting that nobody's work is ever finished. President Nixon fired Morgenthau late in December, 1969, by simply nominating a successor. With much fanfare Morgenthau then became Mayor Lindsay's deputy to clean up the city's narcotics and other crime problems, with a $42,500 salary and a $500,000 budget. Even Lindsay's own ally and running mate, Council President Sanford Garelik, objected. A taxi driver I talked with objected more strenuously. He said that Morgenthau's salary was the equivalent of almost 300,000 subway fares!

The solution to the city's problems must have been simple, because within a matter of weeks Morgenthau, taking a large part of his staff with him, temporarily exited from City Hall to run in the gubernatorial primary for the right to oppose Nelson Rockefeller. His exodus became permanent when he resigned the post during the campaign after the City Council nearly erupted at his conduct. As he launched his campaign, he performed the almost impossible task of uniting such diverse forces as the conservative *Daily News,* the American Civil Liberties Union, and Pete Hamill, of the New York *Post,* against him. They were aghast at his announcement that he would campaign against the political bosses, using information he had gathered while he was United States Attorney. (I was a guest on a radio show and was surprised to discover during a station break that one of the sponsors for that day was the Morgenthau Campaign Committee. The commercial concerned pollution and seemed to equate Morgenthau's nomination with being able to breathe more freely.)

Whenever we had passed each other in a hallway or restaurant over the years, I had thought Morgenthau was emitting in my direction a special glare that he reserved for dangerous public enemies. But during the campaign he hit television, and I discovered that where Browning's last duchess supposedly smiled on all, Morgenthau dispensed his scowl on everyone, rather than on the privileged few. Ben Gross of the *Daily News,* after watching Morgenthau on television, commented that he seemed "annoyed by a distant unpleasant odor." Morgenthau threw in the towel on May 13, 1970, six weeks before the primary was to be held. His supporters blamed lack of funds and a fickle public that believed that issues like the war and rioting deserved more attention than Morgenthau's personal commitment to saving the state.

In any event soon after becoming United States Attorney in 1961, Morgenthau launched his attack on me. While his personal animosity probably stemmed from his father's involvement in the money-plates hearings (something that seemed irrelevant to me but apparently not to him), the fact that he was beholden to Bobby Kennedy was conceivably an issue, too. Remembering his father's problems probably made it easy for him to do enthusiastically to me what Kennedy demanded.

In newspaper interviews Morgenthau has conceded his personal dislike for me but assigned no specific reason. He rested on the comment that one is not immune from prosecution because the prosecutor doesn't like him. He apparently thought this a clever, well-turned phrase, since he repeated it in interviews in such publications as the house organ put out for Diners Club–Fugazy Travel by William Denis Fugazy, whose friendship with Morgenthau came about when he testified for Morgenthau against me in 1963. Others thought it unprofessional for Morgenthau to use his office to vent his personal dislikes.

In a *New York Times* interview a friend of Morgenthau's shed a bit more light on his attitude. He explained that Morgenthau disliked me because he regarded me as a *nouveau riche parvenu,* which at least conveys that he can speak some redundant French, but after he finished with me, I was not all that rich. As to the implications of the phrase—that my family didn't quite make it over on the *Mayflower*—he is correct. But I had thought the only penalty for that was denial of membership in the New York Yacht Club—not admission to jail. Besides, I am rather proud of my family. My grandparents were born in four different European countries, and each chose the United States for a home. My father worked his way through City College and New York Law School at night while teaching during the day. He successively became chief assistant district attorney of Bronx County, county court judge by appointment of Governor Alfred E. Smith, justice of the state supreme court by appointment of Governor Franklin D. Roosevelt, and justice of the appellate division by appointment of Governor Lehman and reappointment by Governors Dewey and Harriman. My mother was an intelligent and gracious lady, whose only cognizable sin was producing me.

II

"The Roy Cohn Case"

SHORTLY AFTER MORGENTHAU was appointed United States Attorney in 1961, I began to receive phone calls from literally dozens of lawyers in New York to tip me off that clients of theirs—most of whom didn't even know me—had been asked by Morgenthau what they could say against me. Potential witnesses or defendants being charged with crimes who were being interrogated on matters totally unrelated to me would be asked whether they knew me and what information they could furnish against me.

"Can you meet me someplace near my office in the Bronx? It's about a personal matter of deep concern to you," said criminal lawyer and textbook author Henry Rothblatt.

My curiosity and apprehension aroused, I asked, "Tell me about it now if you can."

"Over your phone? You must be kidding!"

I met Rothblatt. A client of his (whom I didn't know) was in trouble with the United States Attorney's office. If he could give them some information about me, his troubles would be over.

"I'm representing some clients in a Securities and Exchange Commission problem in Morgenthau's office. They don't know you, but they've been told things will go better for them if they can implicate you in some way"—so advised another prominent attorney.

There were dozens of calls from nonlawyers as well. A client of mine in civil matters, John Van Allen, was involved in a criminal proceeding in the U.S. Attorney's office. Frequently, he would be asked to see the assistant in charge of his case. What could he tell them about me? When he said nothing incriminating, he was taken to the assistant's superiors. When he still demurred, he was told that "this comes right from Morgenthau, and he has the support of the people in Washington." They told Van Allen they were going to take him before the grand jury and "he'd better open up." Finally, in desperation, he called their bluff by saying to them, "Okay. You win. Tell me what you want me to say and I'll say it, even though it's not true." The matter was then dropped.

This investigation heightened when my name came up in the course of a prosecution then in progress by Morgenthau's office. The principal defendants in that trial were archswindler Alexander P. Guterma, president of United Dye and Chemical Corporation, accused of artifically manipulating and illegally trading company stock; Allard Roen, a Las Vegas character and owner of an oil-pipeline company, whose stock he had illegally traded for United Dye; Sam Garfield, convicted gambling-house operator and behind-the-scenes partner of underworld figures; Sidney Barkley, with a long criminal record, who ran a "boiler shop"—a brokerage house that ground out phony stock, which he sold through a high-pressure telephone campaign; and one of their lawyers, Allen K. Swann. Another of their lawyers, Hyman Lehrich, was named as a co-conspirator.

Their criminal manipulation and illegal sale of stock led

to the longest and probably the most expensive criminal trial in legal history. Lasting nearly a year—from February to December, 1962—it took place at Federal Court in New York. It was called the United Dye case, but it became, in the words of Allard Roen, the Roy Cohn case.

The charge was that a handful of conspirators had swindled "thousands of people out of millions of dollars," to quote Robert Morgenthau's assistant, Gerald Walpin, who handled the prosecution. The implications of the case were widespread. It was the classic embodiment of Prosecutor Morgenthau's oft-publicized warning of the invasion of publicly owned companies by racketeers and of "white-collar" crime, the prosecution of which Morgenthau was the self-proclaimed fearless pioneer. But on August 24, 1964, the day fixed for sentencing, Garfield, Roen, Barkley, and Swann received not a single day in jail. One after another they were turned loose by the court on the recommendation of Morgenthau's office! Guterma received no prison sentence in addition to that under his original conviction for issuing false financial statements.

Today, Garfield continues to operate with his old associates; Roen, having sold his interest in the Desert Inn and Stardust casinos to Howard Hughes, rides high as the director of the plush LaCosta Country Club resort near San Diego, California, still in partnership with some of his former associates; Barkley is a familiar figure around Hollywood nightclubs; Swann continues to practice law in Ohio; and master-crook Guterma is wheeling and dealing in Florida. It's as though the United Dye case never happened.

How did the swindlers of thousands of people out of millions of dollars walk out unpunished with Morgenthau's blessing? In view of their past records, he could hardly have believed leniency in order. Nor could he have become doubtful about their guilt. Each one pleaded guilty. Yet on

Morgenthau's recommendation the late Judge William B. Herlands gave each a suspended sentence.

I had known absolutely nothing of the stock fraud, had represented none of the people involved in any way during its commission, and had never owned a share of United Dye stock. Regretfully, however, I had the bad fortune to meet Sam Garfield and Allard Roen when on vacation with a then close friend, William Fugazy, former president of Diners Club—Fugazy Travel. Fugazy did extensive business with Roen's Las Vegas hotels on package tours and promotion. In the cocktail lounge of the Desert Inn he introduced me to Roen and Garfield, who were sort of fixtures there. Just as people ask a doctor on vacation about their ailments, so they ask a lawyer on vacation about their latest legal dilemmas. This was my experience with the Las Vegas group.

Roen, after the United Dye stock sales were over, was called to an interview by a staff member of the Securities and Exchange Commission. He told me he had no attorney at that point (Swann, an out-of-stater, not knowledgeable in criminal law, was himself potentially involved) and asked me if I would request a short adjournment in his behalf. I did so by telephoning the S.E.C. staff lawyer and sending a confirmatory letter. As the United Dye investigation progressed and was ultimately forwarded to the United States Attorney's office in New York, Garfield asked me to inquire into its status and to recommend counsel if necessary. I spoke to the chief of the Criminal Division in the prosecutor's office, who referred me to the assistant handling the case. It turned out that there was a strong possibility that Garfield would be indicted. His best defense to avoid indictment was that he had relied upon advice of his counsel, Swann, in selling his United Dye stock, and it appeared to me important to bring this formally to the attention of the prosecution and the grand jury. Thus I recommended to Garfield that he have counsel—and not me, as I had represented no defendant in a criminal trial since leaving the United States Attorney's office years before. I suggested Murray Gottesman, a seasoned lawyer.

While the case was still before the grand jury, the proper move was to try to prevent an indictment. This is essentially what I was alleged to have done, and a lot of lawyers were up in arms about the charge because the job of a lawyer representing a potential defendant in a criminal case is exactly that: to try to prevent him from being indicted; then if unsuccessful, from being convicted; then if unsuccessful, from being jailed. Certainly it is criminal to bribe a prosecutor to accomplish this, but there was no such charge in my case. The nitty-gritty of our matter was that we tried to do our job in preventing clients from being indicted. I received a fee from Garfield for this and other matters in which I had advised him.

Specifically, Garfield claimed that Swann, his lawyer at the time, told him that the stock could be sold under an exempting regulation. I suggested that Swann explain this to the grand jury. Prior to his appearance, Gottesman and I reviewed Swann's testimony with him at Garfield's suite at the Pierre Hotel.

After this grand-jury investigation, Garfield, Roen, Barkley, Swann, and Lehrich were not named in the indictment, which was returned August 25, 1959. The defendants, among them Guterma and Virgil Dardi, were charged with conspiring to sell United Dye stock fraudulently and with committing mail fraud against people who purchased it.

Shortly after this indictment there was a second one, substantially the same but more artistically drafted. In contrast to the first indictment this one named, among others, Garfield, Roen, Swann, and Barkley.

Now Garfield asked me about a lawyer for the actual trial. He wanted someone well known, and I recommended Milton S. Gould. After preliminary representation by Gould, Garfield and Roen, on the advice of a lawyer friend of theirs, both switched to William Mulligan, a lawyer best known for being ejected from the New York legislative hearings on Communist infiltration in schools, when he represented the left wing of the teachers' union. A widely circulated newspaper photograph showed Mulligan (who was referred to as "Red" Mulligan) being "escorted" out of the legislative hearing room after a raucous diatribe against the committee investigating Communists in the school system. Today, of course, compared with the Chicago Seven and Panther trials, such an incident would cause little excitement. The legal fraternity came to know Mulligan in another connection when he was active in lawyers' activities through the organization of his choice—the National Lawyers Guild, which is listed by the Attorney General as a subversive organization. Needless to say, Mulligan was not a political admirer of mine. (This William Mulligan is not to be confused with William H. Mulligan, the distinguished dean of the Fordham Law School.)

Garfield and Roen could not have found a lawyer more willing to go along with Morgenthau's effort to build a criminal case around the perfectly routine and peripheral relationship I had with Garfield and Roen. My casual connection with them was hardly sinister; the two of them would have to invent something usable if they were to get their desired reward—going scot-free in the United Dye case. They finally came up with a story that the reason they had not been included in the first indictment was that they had bribed Morton S. Robson, the chief assistant United States Attorney, and that I was the one who engineered the bribe.

Here was their story: I was to arrange to keep Garfield and Roen out of the indictment in the United Dye case, which was filed August 25, 1959. I was to accomplish this by bribing someone in the United States Attorney's office. Around Labor Day I telephoned Garfield at the Pierre Hotel in New York.

I told him that the man in the United States Attorney's office who took care of the case would be going to Las Vegas to collect fifty thousand dollars and that he should be given two thirds of it. Garfield said he then called Roen, who was vacationing in California, and said to him: "That fellow from the U.S. Attorney's office who took care of that matter for us is going out to Vegas to collect, and Roy said to give him two thirds of the fifty thousand." Roen said that he would return to Vegas and take care of it—that he had to be back for something else anyway. He must have then snapped his fingers and said: "But, Sam, you forgot to give me the name of this man from the district attorney's office to whom I'm supposed to give the money." Garfield must have snapped his fingers, too, as he replied, "Allard, I forgot to ask Roy his name. I'll call him back and then I'll call *you* back."

According to his story, Garfield then called me and said, "Roy, you forgot to tell me the name of the guy coming out for the money." I said, "Robson." Garfield called Roen back and said, "Robson." The story continued that Roen returned to Vegas, and one balmy fall evening thereafter a man came over to him and said, "I'm Robson," Roen put two thirds of fifty thousand in a "letter-sized envelope," took Robson into the elevator that runs up a couple of floors to a hotel dining room, and handed the envelope to Robson on the way. Garfield says he gave the other one third to me at a later date. (I suppose that when I told Garfield I would inquire at the United States Attorney's office about his case and started off with the chief of the Criminal Division, he mixed it up with the chief assistant, who was Robson and whom I hardly even knew and never spoke with about this case. Roen then followed through with his lurid account of how he paid off Robson on a certain date in Las Vegas.)

As a matter of simple logic, Morgenthau should have realized the idiocy of the suggestion that the second in rank in the most important federal prosecutor's office in the country would go to Las Vegas in the middle of an investigation and personally collect cash from one of the proposed defendants! But apparently Prosecutor Morgenthau was so fond of the story that he failed to check out the facts. If he had, he would have discovered not only that it was palpably false but that it was also provably false.

Robson had never been in Las Vegas in his life. Further, on the day Roen testified he was there, Robson was in New York and could prove it beyond a doubt. He was moving his family from one apartment to another. He not only had witnesses but also had signed receipts covering the move.

Further, it turns out that Robson was not even the one in the United States Attorney's office who made the decision to omit Garfield and Roen from the first United Dye indictment. The decision was made by S. Hazard Gillespie, one of the most distinguished lawyers in the country, who served as president of the New York Bar Association and as Moreland Act Investigating Commissioner by appointment of Governor Rockefeller.

During the grand-jury investigation of me by Morgenthau, based on the Garfield-Roen story, Gillespie was summoned. He immediately explained to Morgenthau that Robson had had absolutely nothing to do with the decision to omit the Garfield-Roen group from the first indictment, but that he, Gillespie, had made the decision because he believed further investigation was necessary to strengthen the case against them. Such further investigation was made under Gillespie's direction, and Garfield and Roen were named as defendants in a superseding indictment approved by Gillespie. Indeed he had not even consulted Robson.

You might assume that Morgenthau would reveal this information to the grand jury that was weighing an indictment against me. Your assumption would be wrong. Not only did Morgenthau never put Gillespie before the grand jury, but he tried to prevent him from testifying at my trial. He actually subpoenaed Gillespie's books and records and threatened to invoke some kind of nonexistent executive privilege against Gillespie if he should attempt to testify. Apparently Morgenthau's theory was that what Gillespie did as United States Attorney and what knowledge came to him during his tenure were state secrets covered by a privilege the executive branch of government has against disclosure, and should Gillespie attempt to testify, Morgenthau's representatives at the trial would assert this "executive" privilege and seek to exclude his testimony.

Gillespie, who, incidentally, had never met me in his life, was not about to be intimidated, and he took the stand at the trial as a defense witness. Homer Bigart, of *The New York Times,* described Gillespie's testimony as "striking at the heart of the Government's case."

Despite his attempts to silence Gillespie, Morgenthau knew he could not make a case of bribery against Robson, me, or anybody else. So he again called me before the grand jury and tried to salvage his crusade by trapping me into a perjury charge. I probably set a record as to the number of questions I was asked—4,851. They covered every phase of my personal and professional life.

I was certain that Morgenthau would come up with an indictment. My assessment was based on the depth of the Morgenthau dislike for me and the encouragement he was undoubtedly receiving at that time from Bobby Kennedy. Toward the final days I had more than a hunch to go on. One of the top members of the Democratic leadership in the House, who President Kennedy knew was a friend of mine, was summoned to the White House one evening shortly before the grand jury expired. The President told him that Morgenthau was insisting on going ahead—saying that he had an iron-clad case against me—and that Bobby was not about to stop him. The congressman sent word of this conversation to me, so I knew for a certainty. But the anticipation turned out to be worse than the event.

On September 3, 1963, the last day of the grand jury's eighteen-month term, a forty-page ten-count indictment was handed up against me—charging not bribery or anything dealing with the 1959 alleged Robson incident but perjury, obstruction of justice, and conspiracy in connection with the current 1962–1963 grand-jury investigation! The perjury was that I lied when I said I met with Garfield, Swann, and Gottesman in 1959 at the Pierre Hotel. The obstruction of justice was that I had told clients and friends who testified before the grand jury that "it is not a crime not to remember." The conspiracy was to commit the perjury and obstruction. A conspiracy, which is an agreement by two or more people to violate a law, is a separate crime in itself. Some judges allow much otherwise inadmissible evidence when there is a conspiracy charge on the theory that each member of the conspiracy is an agent for all the others, so that anything one says binds all the others even if they are not present. For example, if John Doe testified that "Gottesman told me that Roy Cohn said that he was making arrangements to pay off Robson," that is hearsay and inadmissible against me. But if it is charged that I was in a conspiracy with Gottesman, it becomes admissible, as Gottesman is regarded to be my agent. This somewhat tortured doctrine insures the almost ritualistic use of conspiracy counts in indictments by prosecutors. To make the "conspiracy," poor Murray Gottesman was thrown in as a defendant along with me in the conspiracy count.

This was scraping the bottom of the barrel. Without a bribe—which was not charged after investigation—what motive would I have had to commit perjury? And what utter nonsense to make up a story about a meeting with Garfield, Swann, and Gottesman, knowing that two of the three had a deal with Morgenthau and could contradict me in a minute.

I suppose that this type of charge fits into the theory of using any available technicality to "get" someone considered an evil character. The technique has been used in prosecuting alleged Mafia bigwigs for tax evasion. Former Attorney General Kennedy was accused of going after his old enemy Jimmy Hoffa with anything he could use to put him out of commission. This, of course, raises the issue of government of men rather than of law. Do we leave to the unbridled discretion of a temporary incumbent of the Attorney General's or United States Attorney's office the decision as to who should be selected for extinction, and then permit him unfettered use of any technicality to accomplish his aim? The system of selective extinction contradicts the principle that all are entitled to equal treatment and protection under the law. Fortunately, I had the means of fighting back. Many people don't.

In any event all twelve jurors disbelieved the testimony of the witnesses of Morgenthau's side. And this example of the administration of justice netted the taxpayers absolutely zero, after the expenditure of millions of dollars and the use of years of time on the part of judges, prosecutors, grand juries, and juries. (Indeed, because of the sudden death of a juror's father during the jury deliberations—an event that results in a mistrial—my case required two trials.)

When Morgenthau's assistant in his opening statement to the jury at the inception of the eleven-month United Dye trial explained the importance to the administration of justice of convicting Garfield, Roen, Swann, and Barkley, little did he or the jury know that its almost one year of work would go right down the drain one August morning of 1964 when on Morgenthau's recommendation Judge Herlands "walked out," without a day in jail, each and every one of these four major culprits as a reward for their testimony against me, even after that testimony had been soundly rejected by the jury at my trial.

III

"The United States of America Against Roy M. Cohn"

WHEN I WALKED off a plane from Europe on the afternoon of January 17, 1969, a customs agent greeted me: "I'll bet you beat that stiff again, Mr. Cohn." I didn't ask him to explain. I double-timed it to the nearest phone booth in the terminal and called my office. I learned I would be greeted by press, radio, and television as soon as I walked in the door. The news broadcasts announced that Mr. Morgenthau had put me back in the headlines. My previous acquittal had been but a signal for him to try again. I was again facing forty-five years in jail as a result of a six-count indictment he had signed that morning.

The first count charged that six years before, in 1963, I and five others had conspired to "bribe" Bernard Reicher, a former city appraiser, to give information from the city files to help my client, Fifth Avenue Coach Lines, in its then pending condemnation trial. The others charged were John Kiser, one of my law partners at the time; John Curtin, a Philadelphia transit expert; and Reicher—all of whom were indicted as defendants along with me—and Lawrence I. Weisman, former president of Fifth Avenue Coach Lines and Morton Weinberg, former vice-president, who were not named as defendants.

The second and third counts of the indictment named only me as the defendant. They charged that in 1964 I had given three thousand dollars to Reicher through his attorney on a "federal reservation"—the United States Court House—which meant that I could be prosecuted federally. The fourth count was still another conspiracy charge. The defendants were Kiser and I, and we were charged with conspiring to extort Weisman into selling his stock in Fifth Avenue Coach Lines by threatening to expose the fact that he had bribed Reicher, the city appraiser.

The fifth count, essentially a follow-up to the fourth count, charged that we actually extorted Weisman into selling his stock. In the sixth count Kiser and I were charged with "blackmailing" Weisman into selling his stock.

On its face the indictment was absurd. The second part of it completely contradicted its first part. The first part (Counts 1, 2, 3) charged that I had conspired with Weisman to bribe Reicher. If this were true, how could I have extorted Weisman into selling his Fifth Avenue stock by threatening to expose a bribe (Counts 4, 5, 6) that I was involved in myself?

Further, the federal "jurisdiction" was a joke. The offenses charged were state, not federal, offenses; and District Attorney Frank Hogan's office had considered the matter years before and had indicted Reicher, not us.

When Tom Bolan argued to the trial judge close to the end of the case that there was no evidence to support jurisdiction on Counts 2 and 3, the judge agreed but declined to dismiss them, saying that he would instead give a more favorable charge on those counts than he ordinarily would!

Fifth Avenue Coach Lines operated the largest private transit system in the world. It owned and operated over two thousand buses, which dominated surface transportation in New York and Bronx counties. Its revenues exceeded sixty million dollars a year. The management was caught in a political squeeze, resulting from the dependence of Mayor Wagner on the goodwill of Mike Quill, the colorful president of the Transport Workers Union, to which Fifth Avenue's eight thousand bus drivers belonged.

New Year's Eve in New York City always brought "Auld Lang Syne" and the threat of a transit strike by Quill which would paralyze the city. By the time "Auld Lang Syne" was finished the next morning, Quill always ended up with substantial wage increases. Fifth Avenue Coach Lines was not, however, permitted to raise its fare proportionately. The mayor was committed to retention of the fifteen-cent fare —a hot political issue. As city after city around the nation met the cost of living increase with fare rises, New York did not budge. This impasse could only result in financial disaster to Fifth Avenue and its shareholders. As the situation climaxed in 1961, the man who had quietly become Fifth's largest shareholder was a colorful, self-educated multimillionare from Baltimore, named Harry Weinberg.

Weinberg began work as a manual laborer in his early teens, but he soon displayed a remarkable flare for making money. While still a young man, he was able to buy up small parcels of real estate in Baltimore. His success enabled him to acquire the Scranton Transit System. This acquisition was followed by a purchase of the Dallas bus system and the Honolulu Rapid Transit Company.

Weinberg is a dark, stocky man, whose eccentricities are fabled. During a union negotiation in Honolulu, he startled the crowd by transferring his back-and-forth pacing from the floor to the conference table. His hearing is defective in one ear, and when being questioned, such as in a legal case, he will often reply that he didn't know what was going on —the people must have been talking into the wrong ear. As to the way he expresses himself, Casey Stengel is a model of clarity by comparison. Weinberg survives frequent lectures by his Harvard-bred son, Morton, on the evils of his materialism and enjoys watching the young man flop every time he tries something without benefit of his father's materialism. Weinberg is a warm, loyal friend, and he is scrupulous about keeping his word.

In 1960 Weinberg and his interests were the largest shareholders in Fifth. Weinberg's lawyer and close associate from Baltimore was a thirty-three-year-old Harvard law graduate named Lawrence I. Weisman, whom I met one day in 1960 when he came to see me about representing him and Weinberg in their effort to obtain managerial control of Fifth from its worn-out operators. He told me that a prominent New Yorker had suggested he retain Louis Nizer or me, and he had picked me. I did not meet Weinberg until the fight was well under way. Weisman kept telling me to keep him out of the picture, since his image wasn't good. But as I came to know Harry Weinberg, his common sense and sincerity made him more impressive than some of his overeducated detractors.

The "old" management of Fifth was in the hands of a prestigious board that owned virtually no stock in the company. Fifth was long in prestige but short in profits. My firm's investigation showed that large banks and law firms were having a party at the stockholders' expense: While the salaries and expense accounts flourished, there wasn't enough money left to pay dividends. We sued the board and the company. Arrayed against us were some of the largest Wall Street firms.

A key point was our allegation that the non–stock-owning

management was perpetuating its own control of the company by a circular voting device. It had had an affiliate company called Gray Line acquire 24 percent of Fifth Avenue's stock. Fifth Avenue in turn held a 78 percent interest in Gray Line, so that through its control of Gray Line it was able to vote Gray Line's large block of stock in Fifth and assure victory for the old, money-losing management at stockholders' meetings.

As the trial opened before State Supreme Court Justice Henry Epstein, we subpoenaed files from the Bankers Trust Company, which represented the company in certain transactions. After court one day my partner, John Kiser, looked through the files. Buried in one of them was a "confidential" memorandum by one of the bank's top officers about a visit to the bank by Wall Street lawyer Grayson Murphy some years back. The memorandum quoted Murphy as urging the necessity of the continued use of the Gray Line stock device to keep outsiders out of Fifth. Someone apparently forgot to clean out this particular file. Murphy took the stand for the defense and denied ulterior use of the Gray Line device. Armed with his own memorandum to contradict him, I was in the position a prosecutor dreams of. I nailed down Murphy's denial. I then advanced toward the witness chair, holding the memorandum in my hand. I read it to Murphy, then asked him whether his denial was not a complete falsehood. The battery of defense counsel shouted objections as they rose to their feet. The Court asked, "Why do you object?" One of them answered, "That's no way to ask that kind of a question." A sly grin came over Judge Epstein's face as he retorted, "Well, how would you ask it?" We won the case. Parts of it were upset on appeal on legal questions, but by that time Harry Weinberg was president and chairman of Fifth.

Weinberg would not run a losing company. He immediately put into effect certain economies and layed off some personnel. He demanded a fare increase in order to cut the company's losses. Quill countered by calling an illegal strike in March 1962, paralyzing the city as he had done before. Mayor Wagner had two alternatives. He could call off Quill, or he could make Weinberg the goat and blame him for the "crisis." Wagner chose the latter and denounced Weinberg over television as a greedy, inhuman raider whom he would drive out of New York. The mayor declared that he would formally condemn the bus lines, take them away from their private owners, and have the city operate them.

Once this was done, the company and its shareholders were entitled to just compensation for the value of the properties taken. This amount was to be fixed by a valuation lawsuit in the New York courts. We attacked the seizure by condemnation as unconstitutional. I argued the case in the appellate division, a court on which my father had sat for many years. I remember, as the judges retired to deliberate, looking up at my father's name in the glass-domed ceiling, along with the names of other deceased members of the court over the century. The five justices filed into the courtroom and read their decision. They held that the condemnation legislation was unconstitutional. I called Harry Weinberg in Hawaii and told him he might get his buses back, but the legislature, which was in session, quickly passed corrective legislation to conform with the court's decision, and the condemnation was on again.

The valuation proceeding did not involve secrets or surprises; it was simply a listing of the property taken and expert testimony for each side as to its value. The city expert's estimate would be low, and Fifth's higher, and the judge would fix the amount. The most substantial issue in the case was a purely legal one: whether Fifth Avenue was entitled to compensation for its intangible assets, such as operating schedules, training costs for personnel, and the value of its franchises for its bus routes which had been taken away. The trial judge held it was not, and—along with Milton Gould

and Herbert Brownell, who joined with me on the appeal—
we took the case to the Court of Appeals, the state's highest
court. For our intangible assets we won over $20 million in
damages over what had been awarded by the trial court, making a total award of $55 million as against the city's esti-
mate of $18 million. This was probably the most significant
victory in my legal career.

I did not try the original case, though I had very much
wanted to and had made such a request at a meeting with
Harry Weinberg and Larry Weisman in Harry's room at the
St. Moritz Hotel in New York. After listening to both of us,
Harry, who had been pacing up and down the room,
pointed his finger at me and said: "Roy, I believe in you,
and in my opinion you'd win the case. But if you don't, Larry
will never stop rubbing it in and saying we should've gotten
some other lawyers—so let him have his way." Weisman hired
a leading Wall Street firm, and I assumed leadership only after the intangible side had been lost at the trial and the last-
ditch appeal decided upon.

Weisman, who supervised the preparation of the case, hired
as the company's expert witness John Curtin, one of the country's leading transportation engineers. On the city's side was
Bernard Reicher, a spare-parts appraiser, who supervised
the listing of the thousands of spare parts the city had taken
from the company by condemnation. The job was mechani-
cal, and the trial judge directed Reicher for the city and Curtin for the company to work together to accomplish it. They
reached a formal agreement to do so.

The trial was long, and as it was nearing its end in the fall
of 1963, I received a call from longtime Fifth Avenue director
Kenneth Steinreich, who had also served as president of Jacob
Ruppert Brewery and was an outstanding civic leader. Steinreich told me that he had received reliable information that
Weisman had secretly arranged for Fifth Avenue to foot the
bill for a Caribbean cruise taken the previous September by

Reicher and his "wife." Steinreich asked me to look into this immediately, since he felt that the case could be severely damaged if this was true and if it came to light. If the city discovered it after a judgment, a mistrial motion would be a certainty.

I hired an investigator who went to work checking cruise manifests for September, 1962. He came up with nothing. He then allowed for a mistake in date and looked ahead to November and December. The manifest of the *Rotterdam* on December 9, 1962, showed a Mr. and Mrs. Bernard Reicher. Our investigator went to the records and obtained the name of the travel agency through which the cruise had been booked. It was Reliable Travel Service in Brooklyn.

From Reliable's records our investigator ascertained that the bill for the tickets had been paid not by Reicher but by the firm of Curtin, Fifth Avenue's expert witness. Steinreich's information had been correct.

Steinreich and I (I had been a member of the board of directors for a short time between 1962 and 1963) and several other directors of Fifth who were privy to the information decided that a disclosure must be made promptly—we were lucky in that Reicher had not as yet testified for the city. If a disclosure was made prior to his being called, the city would undoubtedly not use him, and a judgment would not be subject to attack for tainted testimony. Some of the directors called for a board meeting to discuss the situation and requested the presence of the senior figure in the Wall Street firm that was acting as Fifth's trial counsel.

By this time—January, 1964—Weisman, in collaboration with Harry Weinberg's son, Morton, had staged a palace revolt and kicked out Harry Weinberg as president and chairman of Fifth and replaced him with himself. Morton had always had the overeducated failure's contempt for the undereducated success. Weisman, knowing that the path we were following would lead to him, attempted to cancel the meeting. On receiving a telegram from four of the directors of the company calling a board meeting for January 20, 1964, Weisman telephoned Steinreich (who had been married to a cousin of Mayor Wagner's until her death many years before) and demanded he meet him in New York. Weisman himself described the way in which he threatened Steinreich at his Hotel Carlyle meeting:

> The first conversation I called Steinreich at the Westchester Country Club where he was then living, or living part-time. I told him that I received a telegram and I suggested that he get into town immediately.
>
> He objected, but agreed to come to town and meet me at the Carlyle.
>
> About two hours later we met at the Carlyle and we continued our conversation. The substance of the conversation was I told Mr. Steinreich I was outraged at his sending the telegram, that if he was going to start exposing improprieties, I was to start exposing that he used the relationship with Mayor Wagner to secure a job as acquisitions chairman of Fifth Avenue Coach at fifteen thousand dollars a year for no work and that I was not going to tolerate this.
>
> I also called his attention to the fact that he had been familiar with the Reicher situation and that this was no surprise to him.
>
> He then said to me that this Reicher situation had gotten to the point where only he through his connections with the city could stop it. He agreed at the end of our conversation to withdraw the telegram.

After this meeting, Weisman himself sent a telegram apparently only to certain of the directors, stating that the directors who had called the meeting had withdrawn their call. Total confusion resulted. Weisman had his rubber-stamp directors stay away to prevent a quorum, but certain outside directors showed up, and an informal meeting was held.

When it became clear that Weisman would be able to delay and possibly prevent the board from properly acting to protect the condemnation case, Steinreich told me to go to Leo Larkin, the city's corporation counsel, and make the disclosure. He suggested it be done away from the Municipal Building. I knew that William Cassidy, the prominent Catholic journalist and educator, was a good friend of Larkin's, so I requested my partner, Tom Bolan, a close friend of Cassidy's, to ask him to arrange a meeting. This he did, and Larkin and I met at Cassidy's Brooklyn apartment on January 21, 1964. I told Larkin what we had found out. The next week he called in the commissioner of investigation, who confirmed our information. Reicher was called before the commissioner and ultimately took the Fifth Amendment. He was discharged from city employ by Larkin on February 3, 1964, and was not used as a witness at the trial. Fifth's case was saved.

If there had been a mistrial or a set-aside verdict, the company could not have escaped bankruptcy during the retrial period. After property is condemned for public use, some years may pass before the amount of money the city owes the owners as just compensation is determined and paid. Recognizing the hardship on the owner of waiting without property and without money, the legislature passed a statute permitting the city to make an "interim" payment of 75 percent of the appraised value of the property. I know of only one instance in which the city has not made this interim payment—Fifth Avenue. (We were never able to get any rational explanation for this occurrence. I mention it because the history of Fifth's shaky financial position is relevant to the charge, which I shall discuss in later pages, that I extorted Larry Weisman into selling his shares.) So after its buses and franchises had been seized and Fifth had no way of bringing in any cash, it still had to meet payrolls, finance the thousands of negligence cases it had been left with, pay charges on bank loans, and so forth. This became a mathematical impossibility, and even without a mistrial, Fifth was in real danger of bankruptcy. The trial had taken a year and a half. If a mistrial had been declared and we had been forced to start from scratch without any interim funds, bankruptcy would have been inevitable. Fortunately, the timing of the disclosure to Larkin was right.

But that was not the end of Reicher. After his discharge by the city, he, with the aid of a lawyer and accountant named Bernard Patrusky, thought they could make some money by blackmail. After leaving Fifth Avenue in early February, 1964, Lawrence Weisman left on a European honeymoon with his second wife. One day his uncle and family lawyer, William Weisman, was contacted by Patrusky and informed that Patrusky's "client," Mr. Reicher, had made a tape some years before of a conversation with Larry Weisman, in which Weisman supposedly made incriminating statements. The tape was played for William Weisman, who found it to be unintelligible, but with Larry unavailable to make the decision he took the safe course and gave Patrusky five thousand dollars cash, which was taken out of the savings account of Larry's parents in Baltimore.

Patrusky made a similar attempt against Morton Weinberg, who did not pay but referred him to me. This was all in the spring of 1964 after Reicher was no longer in the city's employ. During this period Weinberg and Weisman had sold their Fifth Avenue holdings to a company controlled by Edward Krock and Victor Muscat. (Weinberg had long wanted to sell. He had made his investment in Fifth to run a transit company and not to buy a lawsuit, as he put it. So when the Krock-Muscat offer came, he was ready to do business.)

The Krock-Muscat business marriage united two disparate individuals, who shared one thing—greed for more money. Krock had been a "liquidator" during the depression, and he learned to be able to walk into a deserted machine shop and by scanning the floor form a judgment as to the shop's resale value. After the necessary payoffs he would acquire the plant and liquidate it by selling off everything inside. Having stripped the plant, he might sell the shell to the longtime watchman for his life savings, knowing that the watchman had always seen the owners living in luxury from the operation of the plant. It was a tough business—getting rich on other people's poverty. But Krock became tough. A vain man, he wears only blue shirts and ties to bring out the blue in his eyes. Man-Tan gives him the semblance of a perpetual suntan. Krock's financial pecadillos were fantastic. Among his quick tricks was his habit of taking duplicate repayments of sums he advanced to public companies (always with a handsome bonus) and forgetting to repay the duplicate for a year or so —$175,000 in one instance.

When my law associate, Tom Bolan, became president of Fifth Avenue, he instituted a suit against Krock to recover moneys he had taken. Krock was indicted for false S.E.C. filings and pleaded guilty during my trial in 1969. While milking the till on the one hand, he was the political big shot on the other. A friend of Ambassador Joseph P. Kennedy's, he constantly bragged about the "$100,000 cash" he gave John Kennedy's presidential campaign.

Muscat is a different type. Nothing seems to faze him. Everyone with whom he does business is an object to be taken. It is all a game. Muscat was indicted in June, 1969, for perjury and false S.E.C. filings. He never went to trial, but he made a deal to plead guilty and receive extreme leniency in return for testifying against me.

At this point Weisman was guilty of having engineered a payoff to Reicher, a city witness; and Reicher—with Patrusky—of a successful shakedown of Weisman.

From here on in, it was the United Dye story all over again. Discovering the Reicher incident did not require the ultimate in detective work on Morgenthau's part. After his discharge in 1964 as a result of my disclosure to Corporation Counsel Larkin, it had been front-paged in *The New York Times*. But

Morgenthau apparently decided that he would try to tie me into it in some way and make another criminal case against me. He went about it by calling Weisman before a 1968 grand jury. Weisman retained counsel who went to see Morgenthau personally to find out what it was all about. The lawyer reported back to Weisman that Morgenthau said he had an open-and-shut case against Weisman for having bribed Reicher. But Morgenthau did not care about Weisman; his paramount interest was Roy Cohn. What could Weisman say that would incriminate Cohn?

Weisman was ready to negotiate the deal but he was not going to settle for a suspended sentence, as had Garfield and Roen. He wanted formal immunity from prosecution for any crime he had ever committed. Morgenthau agreed, subject to one condition. Before he gave Weisman immunity, Weisman would have to have an off-the-record session and tell Morgenthau's office exactly how far he would go in talking about me. The best Weisman could come up with was a claim that *after* he had authorized payment for the Reicher cruise, he had told me about it and that I had said, "How stupid can you be to do something like that by check?" He expanded his story by saying that I also knew of other payments to Reicher.

Morgenthau must have realized he would have a Herculean task in trying to make Weisman's allegations stick. If I had been party to a bribe to Reicher, why would I have been the one to go to the city's corporation counsel and tip him off to something that would incriminate me? Undeterred by this flaw, Morgenthau determined to bolster up his case by adding a second and novel charge that went this way: By letting Weisman know I knew of the Reicher incident and was about to go to the city's lawyer to expose it, I was in effect extorting Weisman into getting out of Fifth Avenue under threat of exposure of the Reicher incident if he didn't. Weisman did sell out his Fifth position—on January 29, 1964. To sustain Morgenthau's theory, it would have been essential that my disclosure to Larkin was not until after that, because if

I had done it before and Weisman knew I had, there would be nothing left with which to threaten and extort Weisman into selling.

To overcome this problem, Morgenthau's office decided to contend that I had not gone to see Larkin until January 30, 1964—after Weisman was out of Fifth—and that I had done so then because too much had gotten around about the incident. Morgenthau believed that the indictment would be strengthened by adding to the Reicher incident charges that I had criminally extorted Weisman into selling his holdings in Fifth Avenue.

The head of my law firm is forty-five-year-old Thomas A. Bolan, an Army Air Force ace in World War II, who worked his way through college and law school, graduating first in his class in each, and since then a Knight of Malta and judge advocate of the Catholic War Veterans. Tom, who served as a federal prosecutor, is quiet but shrewd and tough.

Tom was next to me on the morning of September 23, 1969, as the clerk called for trial "The United States of America against Roy M. Cohn, John Curtin, and John A. Kiser." He predicted that Weisman would be Morgenthau's first witness. He was right, and Morgenthau's case went up in smoke.

Weisman admitted under cross-examination that rather than having been criminally extorted to sell his Fifth Avenue shares, he had sold them at an enormous financial profit to himself. He conceded that he had paid only fourteen dollars per share and sold out for thirty per share to Krock and Muscat, a profit of over a quarter of a million dollars on the stock alone. He further conceded that he had not even paid for the stock but had given notes for it to Harry Weinberg, which were coming due shortly. As part of his agreement to sell, Weisman had successfully demanded that his Baltimore law firm receive over $100,000 in additional fees, that an employment contract he had voted to himself shortly before be bought up for its full amount of $145,000, and that he receive $25,000 for deferred compensation—a package of over one million dollars with pure profit to him of over half a million!

Weisman further admitted that he was afraid Fifth couldn't stay solvent until the condemnation award came through and that his mentor, Harry Weinberg, who owned three times the stock Weisman did, was selling out to Krock and Muscat, so that Weisman's tenure as head of Fifth was shaky at best. If ever a man did not need to be criminally extorted to sell out, it was Weisman.

Another feature of Weisman's testimony made the charge even more ludicrous. If someone criminally extorts and threatens you, you call the police or at least run the other way when you see your extorter approaching. So, Weisman's conduct toward me after the alleged criminal extortion proved to be most interesting to the jury. We produced a hand-written letter from Weisman to me shortly after the claimed extortion. Along with birthday greetings to me, he chided me for not returning his phone calls and said he regarded me as one of his dearest personal friends and hoped I would be such always. We then related series of events revolving around his marital life.

For present purposes, I shall refer to his wives as Mrs. Weisman I, II, III, and IV. By the time of the alleged extortion in January, 1964, Mrs. Weisman I had been divorced and left with their child in Baltimore, and Larry was making plans to take an extensive European trip with a young lady he had met in New York. On the eve of sailing the young lady became Mrs. Weisman II and went off to Europe with Larry. The trip over and the purpose of the marriage having been served, Mrs. Weisman II was disembarked and soon became another former Mrs. Weisman. The stage was now set for Mrs. Weisman III, whom Larry married in an elaborate church ceremony in the spring of 1967. She soon suspected Larry of playing around and also alleged that he had beaten her. After a session at a marriage counselor's office, Larry left for Hawaii. On his return he found the lock on the apartment door changed and his clothes left in suitcases in the lobby of the building—courtesy of Mrs. Weisman III, who could not wait to become the third former Mrs. Weisman. Between my indictment and the trial, Larry broke his engagement to the leading candidate to become the new Mrs. Weisman and married another, who thus became Mrs. Weisman IV and frequently graced the courtroom in her miniskirts.

The relevance of these lovely ladies to Mr. Morgenthau's indictment of me for having criminally extorted Larry Weisman in January, 1964, lies in the fact that the various entanglements, disentanglements, and children along the way were not without legal complication. In addition to the routine divorce trials and custody suits, a surprised Larry, while on a visit to Baltimore in April, 1968, found himself in the city jail for nonsupport of his child by Mrs. Weisman I. Throughout all these trials and tribulations the one to whom Larry turned for assistance was the man Morgenthau was trying to send to jail for having criminally extorted Larry—myself.

The relationship was not just legal. After my allegedly having extorted him, he invited me to his 1967 church wedding. When Mrs. Weisman III put him out on the street, he left his clothes at my home. And—the *pièce de résistance* —only weeks before agreeing to tell a story that I had extorted him (in return for immunity from Morgenthau), Weisman presented me with an inscribed silver pitcher and twelve cups. The inscription read:

R M C

To the Second Best Lawyer
In the United States
With Regard and Affection
of
LIW—No. 1

We concluded Weisman's cross-examination by unveiling in front of the jury this gift presented to his extorter.

How did Morgenthau fall into the trap? How could he have believed that a jury would buy a story of blackmail in which the victim makes half a million? It goes back to his seeming refusal to look at anything inconsistent with whatever negative statement anyone might make about me.

Weisman was the prosecution's first witness. Their last one was Bernard Patrusky, the lawyer-accountant for Bernard Reicher who had shaken down Weisman's uncle for five thousand dollars and had attempted the same with Morton Weinberg.

After Reicher's discharge by the city as a result of my visit with Larkin, he was indicted by District Attorney Hogan's office for perjury and grand larceny in having submitted phony vouchers to the city, listing, for example, all sorts of hours of work on the condemnation case by him and his girl friend when, in fact, they were off on the Caribbean cruise. And he had admitted having taken all sorts of moneys from Weisman and Morton Weinberg, so he was obviously willing to tell any story that Morgenthau encouraged. So was Patrusky. He needed to avoid prosecution for perjury and for the shakedown. But the story they concocted was as inherently impossible as Weisman's. I was charged with having paid bribe money to Patrusky for Reicher in March and June of 1964—months *after* Reicher was fired by the city and no longer in a position to turn over anything to Fifth Avenue. Indeed, the whole trial was over in the condemnation before his bribe payments were allegedly made. Further, why would I bribe someone who was fired because I complained about his conduct to his boss? Once again, the whole thing made no sense, but Morgenthau went ahead anyway.

The prosecution must have saved Patrusky for the last because they thought he'd make such a good witness. His story was that I had given him money for Reicher at my office in March, 1964, and then again right outside Courtroom 110, where I was on trial in the first Morgenthau indictment on June 16, 1964. Patrusky's fabrications were ostensibly well tailored. I could not say I was out of town on June 16, 1964, when everyone knew I was a defendant in court. So he thought he was safe in lying. His problem stemmed from the fact that he couldn't stop with a simple lie—he had to "embellish," as he once put it. So when he described the March "payment," he detailed a concomitant conversation he had with me in which I told him we had bought the Tyson-Sullivan Theatre Ticket Agencies. He had probably read that we had but forgot to check his dates, which would have showed that Tyson was not purchased until the next fall and that no such conversation as he described could have taken place.

He slipped similarly on the second "payment." Not satisfied with having said it took place outside the courtroom on the morning of June 16, 1964, he went on to "embellish" with details, such as which witness was being cross-examined as he entered the courtroom. I imagine he culled this embellishment material from newspaper and magazine reports of my first trial, with a helping hand from Morgenthau's assistants. He slipped here because the witness he referred to was not being cross-examined on that morning, and we produced the court records and my lawyer, Frank Raichle, to prove it. Patrusky was thus discredited on both claimed payments.

Edward Garlock, who represented John Kiser, told the jury:

> What emerged from my reflections on the course of this case . . . was fairly ugly but demonstrable. . . . The prosecution did what no scientist, what no good investigator, what no seeker of truth, does—or has any right to do. What they did

here was to start with a fixed assumption of guilt and proceeded from that point to tailor and select the evidence that
they would present to support that hypothesis.

Now why did they do that?

Perhaps that original error, that original sin, stemmed from
the paramount interest of the United States Attorney in Mr.
Cohn. . . .

They selected, they tailored the evidence that they wanted
which would support their objective, and they ignored, withheld, or sought to suppress the evidence which would tend to
disprove what they wanted to establish.

IV

Witnesses for
the Prosecution

FOR THE YOUNG we are living in the Age of Aquarius. In legal circles it is the age of the accomplice witness. An accomplice is one who himself participated in the commission of the crime charged. After being caught, he becomes an accomplice witness if he makes a deal with the prosecutors to testify against his former partners in crime in return for lenient treatment for himself.

We are told that this practice is essential in detecting and punishing crime. Many a prosecutor has argued to the jury that were it not for accomplice testimony, criminals could not be brought to the bar of justice. And who can know what goes on in the course of a criminal act better than an actual participant?

Implicit in this reasoning is that the prosecutor makes his deal with the less culpable in order to bring to justice the more culpable. Thus, a deal can be justifiably made with one who possessed stolen goods if he will make possible the apprehension of the one who actually did the stealing. The driver of the getaway car can be dealt with if he will give up the actual armed robbers. And a deal can readily be made by the "John" in a vice-squad raid if he will be so unchivalrous as to testify against the professional young lady who was the beneficiary of his economic largess in return for her salable commodities. This is the rationale: Deal with the one on the fringes to catch the ones more directly responsible.

In neither of my cases was even this rationale valid. For in each, Morgenthau made deals with the actual perpetrators of the crimes in an attempt to pull me in from the sidelines. Garfield, Roen, Swann, and Barkley—all convicted of swindling—were permitted to escape jail by helping Morgenthau try me for "obstructing" his investigation of me. In the 1969 trial Reicher and Patrusky, who admitted taking bribe payments and committing blackmail, and Weisman and Morton Weinberg, who admitted having paid the bribes, all escaped jail for saying that when I heard about Reicher's Caribbean cruise, I commented to them that it was stupid to do things like that by check.

For that, I was indicted, supposedly by a grand jury but actually by the prosecutor who decides whom the grand jury should indict. It is the prosecutor who makes the deals, and in my cases Morgenthau clearly did not trade the less culpable for the more culpable. In the interests of getting me he traded with twelve swindlers and crooks.

As for the credibility of such witnesses, the prosecutor invariably notes that the defendant, not the prosecution, chose him as his friend and confidant. This is all well and good as long as the accomplice witness is not lying—but lying becomes almost a new profession for many of them. Twelve out of twelve major witnesses who testified against me in the two trials were accomplice witnesses.

Two of the recent celebrities in this area have been Joe

Valachi, the former Mafia leader who has blown the whistle on the rest of the boys (and after whom one of my friends has named her canary), and Herbert Itkin, who made hundreds of thousands of dollars out of bribery schemes, kept his ill-gotten gains virtually with official sanction, and then turned in those he claims to have dealt with. He is best known for his testimony against Carmine DeSapio. Itkin, with obvious relish, told how he got money to "bribe" officials, pocketed it, and gave the government agencies the empty bank wrappers to use as evidence.

Itkin's capacity for prevarication is enormous. I was at a party with some *New York Times* reporters one evening in 1968. One to whom Morgenthau had been leaking the "inside" about what Itkin was saying and who had interviewed Itkin himself greeted me with: "Gee, I didn't know you knew Herbie Itkin so well. He's been telling me all about it." This astounded me. Until the publicity about his being an informer appeared, I hardly knew Itkin's name. The only contact I could recall was that a law partner of his represented some hoodlum whom a client of mine had sued for separation in New York State Supreme Court years before. When I told this to the reporter, he said, "I'm interested to hear it, because to hear Itkin talk, he's your best friend." This same reporter, by the way, accurately predicted the contents and number of counts in my "next" indictment, having been given an "off-the-record" detailed rundown by that champion of right of privacy and grand-jury secrecy —Bob Morgenthau. One of the other reporters commented, "Morgenthau is a real *yenta*. He loves to leak out what he's got lined up for his list—on which you occupy first position."

Morgenthau and Itkin sounded like a match made in heaven. In fact, in late 1969, when Morgenthau gave an interview to *The New York Times* outlining the disaster that would befall America if President Nixon were permitted to replace him, he cited as a witness to his own indispensability none other than Herbie Itkin. "I had to promise Herbert Itkin a dozen times that I wouldn't be leaving before he agreed to testify in the DeSapio case," Morgenthau said. Apparently the President determined that Itkin was not the appropriate forum through which to channel top Justice Department appointments for approval.

New York State law requires corroboration and does not permit conviction on the testimony of an accomplice witness standing alone, because of its inherent unreliability. Federal law does, and it should be changed.

Bernard Patrusky provides a perfect example of the accomplice witness. He is a lawyer and an accountant in his mid-thirties, with a swarthy complexion and a stocky build. He gives the impression of a shady character but is the kind of smooth talker made to be a perfect con man. He was an ideal associate for Bernard Reicher, a crude and unscrupulous man.

A background check of Patrusky did not reveal very much. This disturbed us, since he was about the only major witness against me whose past activities were a mystery. From what we heard from people who knew him, we were sure he was an unsavory character, but we could not establish anything specific. "The only one who worries me in this whole picture is Patrusky," Myron J. Greene, the lawyer who handled the preliminary trial matters, said not once but constantly. He was right. Tom Bolan and I kept shaking our heads and saying to each other, "We're missing the boat on Patrusky. There has to be something there." There sure was.

I have learned to accept all telephone calls even if I don't know the caller. They often lead to important information. My trial counsel, Joseph E. Brill, has the same policy, which is how he uncovered a witness who was instrumental in the acquittal in the Brannigan murder trial. During the first week of my trial Brill returned to his office after court. "A man named Rudolph Johnson called me," he said. "He said

Patrusky and Reicher are a pair of blackmailers, and he has documentary proof of it. I'm going to see Johnson tomorrow." We crossed our fingers. Maybe this was the break we had been waiting for. Late the next afternoon, a six-foot-four massively built Negro appeared at Mr. Brill's office. He was Rudolph Johnson.

"Reicher is the biggest crook and swindler I ever met. He fleeced me for a fortune, and Patrusky was his partner" were Johnson's first words as he took the chair opposite Brill's desk. "Relax and tell me about it," Brill replied. Later that evening Brill reported: "Johnson unfolded one of the strangest tales of blackmail and thievery I ever heard. It seems that Johnson, through a Swiss corporation, started an import-export business in Ghana. Johnson lived in Paris. Somehow or other, he met up with Bernard Reicher. Reicher persuaded him to let him run the export-import business. Reicher went to Accra, the capital of Ghana, to take charge of the business. Within a short time Johnson discovered that Reicher was making unauthorized personal expenditures and that there were financial irregularities. On learning that Johnson was suspicious, Reicher wrote him an indignant letter of resignation. Johnson thought that was the end of Reicher's activities in Ghana. But he soon received quite a shock. After Reicher wrote his letter of resignation, he remained in Accra and literally cleaned out the company's bank account. He drew out about forty thousand dollars." Brill went on: "Johnson told me he retained counsel in Ghana, a formal complaint was filed, and Reicher was arrested. But after bail was set, Reicher jumped bail."

Tom said: "If we can prove this, it's great so far as Reicher is concerned, but I am disappointed at not having heard Patrusky's name mentioned. I thought he was involved in this." Brill smiled as he replied: "Give me a chance, I'm just about to get to that. Johnson said that Reicher was a blackmailer in addition to being a thief and that things reached such a pitch that Johnson had one of his Swiss associates, Freddie Bloom, telephone Reicher in New York. The call was taken not by Reicher but by Patrusky. In the course of conversation Patrusky told that he was Reicher's partner and fully familiar with the Ghana business. Patrusky nursed Bloom along by agreeing with him that Reicher was a blackmailer and saying he should be behind bars. But, Johnson continued, Patrusky attempted some blackmail of his own and tried to convince Bloom that it would be in his own best interests to come quickly to New York and straighten matters out with Patrusky."

The significance of this for us was monumental. Here we had proof of the two principal prosecution witnesses on the bribery part of my case having been partners in a blackmail scheme, which also resulted in the embezzlement of moneys from Johnson's company. If Johnson's story held up, Patrusky and Reicher would be exposed under cross-examination not only as blackmailers but as partners in the game. Then came the big question. I asked it. "How do we know we can believe Johnson?"

Brill said, "I believe him. The story rings true, but most important, he claims to have tangible proof." Brill turned to Bolan: "Tom, I want you to meet him tomorrow. He says he will bring the proof." There followed a series of meetings between Tom and Johnson at an East Side cafeteria. When Tom returned from one of them, he walked into my office smiling. "You must live right," he said. "The story is true, and I have seen the proof. Not only does Johnson have Reicher's letter and the checks he wrote when he cleaned out the bank account, but he has an actual tape recording of Bloom's overseas telephone conversation with Patrusky. I have heard it and it is dynamite."

On that Saturday afternoon we played the tape recording in the presence of Dick Owen, who was representing my co-defendant John Curtin, and Ed Garlock. It was incredible.

It started with the overseas operator asking for Reicher, and Patrusky insisting that he would take the call. Then Patrusky's voice came over loud and clear, and the import of the conversation was just as Johnson had described it. Patrusky readily agreed with Bloom that Reicher was a blackmailer who belonged in jail.

> BLOOM: This is called—this is called blackmail over this side of the ocean, and it's usually sentenced by seven years in prison—in this side anyway of the ocean.
> PATRUSKY: Well, if he came back here, we could do the same thing to him.

Patrusky then used one of the usual tricks from a con man's grab bag by posing as a big power in governmental affairs.

> PATRUSKY: Tell Mr. Johnson that I will keep his passport in full effect as I did to get it for him. . . . And Mr. Reicher had attempted to revoke it. I prevented that from happening.
> BLOOM: Look, it's a strange country, your country, when you tell—where people can revoke passports of third parties, but that's a comment of, of—
> PATRUSKY: Mr. Bloom, every country has people in certain authoritative positions.
> BLOOM: Yes.
> PATRUSKY: I occupy that position here.

We all agreed that this was clearly admissible on cross-examination as to both credibility and evidence of the partnership in blackmail between Patrusky and Reicher. But Tom did not want to leave anything open to question. He suggested we locate the barrister who filed the complaint in Ghana and bring him to the United States with a certified copy of Reicher's arrest record and the facts on his bail-jumping. He brushed aside my concern about the expense, and I realized he was right. The lawyer was located and agreed to come. We now awaited Patrusky's appearance on the witness stand with confidence.

When Patrusky was called before the grand jury in December, 1968, he must have wondered which of his "deals" was being investigated. The questioning soon made it apparent that it was his collaboration with Reicher in successfully blackmailing Larry Weisman's uncle. A worried man, Patrusky retained a former assistant prosecutor now in private practice to find out what could be done. The lawyer went to Morgenthau's office. The solution would be simple: Let Patrusky implicate me, and his blackmailing activities and perjury before the grand jury would be overlooked. As he put it on the witness stand: " . . . He [his lawyer] told me that they [Morgenthau's assistants] were understanding people, and that they were reasonable people."

> QUESTION: Didn't he also say, "Don't worry"?
> ANSWER: Yes, he did.

Patrusky was now ready to become an accomplice witness against me, prepared to tell whatever lies were necessary to buy his own way out.

The whole relationship between him and Morgenthau's office changed overnight. In his December grand-jury appearance, before he became an accomplice witness, he was describing a recent trip in from Brooklyn when Paul Perito, one of Morgenthau's assistants, interrupted to suggest: "Didn't you think of jumping off the bridge?" But after that the deal was made and Patrusky returned to the January grand jury to attempt to bury me, Perito's only interruption was to solicitously inquire as to whether Patrusky didn't wish to smoke and relax. Patrusky later proudly announced from the stand that he and Morgenthau's assistants prosecuting me were on a first-name basis: "I have had occasion

to call every one of those gentlemen by their first names."
Patrusky climbed from blackmailer and perjurer to the prosecutor's treasured ally in one easy lesson.

On direct examination Patrusky exuded confidence. He
smiled broadly; his answers were like lectures to the jury and
counsel from a smug instructor. Late in the afternoon of his
first day of cross-examination, however, my lawyer, Joe Brill,
wiped the smile off Patrusky's face. He faced Patrusky and
asked: "Do you remember having a conversation with a man
named Freddie Bloom in which you said something about
Reicher engaging in blackmail?"

> PATRUSKY: That name is not familiar to me at this moment.
> BRILL: Has it been familiar to you at prior times or moments?
> PATRUSKY: I don't recall that name.
> BRILL: Would your recollection be refreshed by any recording
>   of any conversation that you had with Freddie Bloom?
>
> .   .   .
>
> THE COURT: The witness is telling me that he recalls who
>   Freddie Bloom is.
> PATRUSKY: Is this a gentleman from Switzerland?

The jurors were literally on the edges of their seats, hanging on every word and watching Patrusky's reaction. But
the judge, Inzer B. Wyatt, rang down the curtain. He
wanted to hear the tape recording first. We recessed until
the next morning and went into Wyatt's robing room to listen. Even John Allee, another Morgenthau assistant, and Perito seemed amazed and bewildered at what they heard.

After hearing the recording, Judge Wyatt wondered what
it had to do with the case! He excluded the recording but
did so in such a way that it redounded to our benefit. He
told the jury:

> Now, Mr. Foreman, ladies and gentlemen of the jury, you
> will remember yesterday afternoon that during the questioning

of Mr. Patrusky he was asked whether he remembered a conversation with a man named Freddie Bloom in which he,
Patrusky, said something about Reicher engaging in blackmail.

Now, I assumed that the question referred to Reicher engaging in blackmail in connection with the Fifth Avenue
Coach Lines. . . .

So the judge said in effect that he would not let the jury hear
the tape because it dealt with another blackmail scheme, not
with this one.

Two things characteristically happen to accomplice witnesses. First, they begin to enjoy their roles. They are artists
performing, and they will spare nothing to turn in a stellar
performance. And second, they begin to "embellish" their
testimony. As I mentioned earlier, the word "embellish"
(when I was summing up the case, I read a dictionary defini-
tion of it to the jury: "to add details of a fictitious story")
was Patrusky's, not mine. Patrusky asked Perito before the
grand jury whether he should embellish any of his answers.
A witness like this cannot help embellishing his answers and
adding details, and this is often how a good cross-examiner
can expose him for what he is. That is what happened to Patrusky at my trial.

Whereas Reicher claimed he had gotten money from Patrusky who said he collected it from me, the prosecution brought
out on Reicher's direct examination that he had paid no tax
on any such moneys. This was brought out on direct to take
the sting out of Mr. Brill eliciting on cross-examination that
Reicher had never reported any such moneys, making him
either an admitted tax evader, a liar, or both. Not so on Patrusky's direct. He eagerly testified that he had received
moneys from me for Reicher and that he had kept 30 percent
as a "collection fee." Part of his psyche was to cast himself
in the role of a lawyer merely handling a legitimate collection
claim. But the prosecution did not have him say, as they did

Reicher, that he had failed to report his share on his tax returns. At this, a good cross-examiner would at once smell a rat. He would figure he was being baited into asking Patrusky whether he had recorded receipt of any such moneys and whether he had reported them on his income-tax returns. And by all odds, Patrusky, all prepared, would grin and answer: "I sure did record and report the moneys, and here are my work papers and tax return showing them." Most cross-examiners, drawing upon the rule that one does not ask a question unless he knows what the answer will be, would not have taken the chance. But Mr. Brill, Tom, and I decided we would—rule or no rule.

We reasoned that since I had never given him such money, any record he produced must be a forgery. So we went gung-ho. Brill asked Patrusky whether in 1964 he kept records for cash and check transactions. Answer: Of course, he did. Did his cash records reflect money he says I gave him? Along came the anticipated grin, and Patrusky gleefully blurted out, "Of course, they do. My 1964 work sheet has it right there, and so does my tax return." Brill asked for the records. Patrusky said he had been afraid to leave them with Perito but would gladly bring them in the next day. Before lunch the next day Patrusky left the witness stand and came back with a briefcase from which he extracted and proudly displayed a penciled accountant's work sheet headed "1964," containing an item for cash fees from B. Reicher.

We examined the document at Gasner's Restaurant at lunch hour and were sure it was a fraud. I quickly initiated contact with a retired FBI questioned-documents examiner in Washington. He said the work sheet could be examined for age and that if the watermark on the paper was not in use until after 1964, we were in business. When we returned to court for the afternoon session, Patrusky gladly "embellished" his testimony by adding that the actual writing on the work sheets was done in 1964 by his partner, Herbie Weinstein, who while doing it in 1964 had before him "the canceled checks, the checkbooks, and me." But as Patrusky was to leave the stand, something revealing occurred. He wanted to take away from court with him his "1964" work paper. Now I knew it had to be a phony. Why in late 1969 would he be so worried about leaving a five-year-old useless-to-him work paper in court for a few days? I nudged Joe and Tom, who had the same reaction. We objected to its leaving the courthouse, and it was placed in the custody of the clerk as exhibit X. Patrusky then left the stand as the final prosecution witness, and Prosecutor Allee rose to his feet to announce grandly, "The United States of America rests."

I turned around half expecting to see battalions from National Guard units of each of the fifty states march in to the tune of "Battle Hymn of the Republic" and take me outside to face a firing squad.

After Patrusky left the courtroom, we specifically stated that we were going to have the work sheet examined for age. Court broke up about 5 P.M. An hour later Patrusky telephoned Allee and again asked him about when he would get back his work paper. Allee told him that it was being held because the defense were going to have it examined for age. Five minutes later Patrusky appeared in Morgenthau's offices. He had made the dash from his office several blocks away from the courthouse so fast that as I told the jury in summation, you could've played cards on his coattails. Patrusky told Allee that the age examination was unnecessary. The work sheet had not been prepared in 1964, as he had testified, but had been manufactured in 1969, on the eve of my trial! I don't think that that part of the United States of America that was being represented by Morgenthau rested well that night.

Patrusky, the embellisher, was down but not out. He had an explanation. His partner, Herbie Weinstein, had been behind in his work, and although Patrusky had thought the work sheet had been prepared in 1964, Weinstein had been embarrassed to tell him until 6 P.M. that night that it had not been prepared until the eve of trial. Of course, Patrusky had said the day before that he, personally, had been with Weinstein when the work sheet was prepared years before. (Remember, in preparing it Weinstein had before him "the canceled checks, the checkbooks, and me.")

The scene in the judge's chamber the next morning was pandemonium. We demanded that Patrusky be brought back before the jury for further cross so the fraud could be disclosed. At no time did Allee volunteer to bring Patrusky back on the stand or even suggest this procedure. Allee favored calling Weinstein to the stand to "explain," but as Allee knew, Weinstein was busily consulting both his lawyer and his doctor. Chances of Weinstein's showing up ranged from slim to none. It was Joe Brill and Tom Bolan who demanded that Patrusky be recalled to the stand. And it is lucky that they did, because Weinstein never did appear. However, his doctor visited the courtroom and at least provided some comic relief.

Judge Wyatt is a great believer in making United States marshals earn their pay. He will order them into action on a moment's notice. When Ed Garlock had difficulty in getting some of the character witnesses he was calling to testify for John Kiser to come into New York the Friday of the Thanksgiving weekend, Judge Wyatt promptly volunteered to "send the marshal" out to bring them in. Garlock had reservations about the reaction of the character witnesses, who were former Governor Robert Meyner and other prominent public personages, at being taken into custody by the marshal and brought to court, so he declined the judge's offer. No such declination was forthcoming in the case of Herbie Weinstein's physician, Dr. Philip Aronowitz. Judge Wyatt was anxious to move forward, and when told that Weinstein might not be up to appearing but that his doctor was out on house calls, the judge contemplated issuing a bench warrant for the doctor and sending out the marshal to get him. The warrant wasn't issued, but the marshal was, and he produced the good doctor in court late that afternoon.

Dr. Aronowitz was like the old comedy-skit character Dr. Cronkite. A little man, he popped around the witness stand and answered such questions as: "Would Weinstein be scared if he had to testify here?" with "Why, I'm not Weinstein and I'm scared." Ed Garlock has a lot of medical knowledge, his brother having been the famous surgeon Dr. John Garlock. So he cross-examined Dr. Aronowitz and elicited the fact that the doctor was not a heart specialist, had received no referral file or information from the specialist who had taken care of Weinstein, and had not seen Weinstein for his condition in some months. Later on, when a heart specialist commissioned to do a report of Weinstein's condition was very late in sending it in, Garlock raised a fuss. The judge allowed that it didn't make much difference, since he had already heard one doctor on Weinstein—namely, Dr. Aronowitz. When Garlock belittled the value of this, the following exchange occurred:

THE COURT: I thought myself that he [Weinstein's doctor] was a rather impressive character.
GARLOCK: I thought he was amusing and interesting, but he was hardly qualified.
THE COURT: I mean candid, frank, straightforward, truthful, well informed, disinterested, objective. Your impression of him and mine is completely different.

Having apparently exhausted his supply of laudatory adjectives, the Court slumped back in his chair. Garlock rose and said, "I agree with all of that except I didn't think he was competent, your Honor." The spectators broke up.

In any event we got Patrusky back on the stand on Monday morning. After telling his new story he insisted that the information on the phony work sheet was still accurate, because Weinstein had prepared it from notes he had made in 1964.

Where were the notes? Oh, Weinstein "destroyed" them a few weeks ago after making up the exhibit. Well, then, where were the 1964 records testified to by Patrusky as having formed the basis for the transaction? Patrusky—still down but still not out—said exasperatedly, as though everyone had to understand, that because of overcrowding in the office files in 1966, some of the records, including these, were to be moved to Weinstein's home, and he put them in the trunk of his car for this purpose. However, his wife left the car in front of a supermarket, and while she was shopping, the car was stolen. It was recovered a few days later, but—guess what?—none other than the very records we wanted had been stolen from the trunk, and if we didn't believe it, the loss had been reported to the insurance company!

Perito lamely got up and waved a form in the air, representing it as the insurance form that would corroborate Patrusky's story. Now we were out for blood. We distrusted the authenticity of anything connected with Patrusky. We asked to see the insurance form. It was like pulling molasses to get it away from Perito. It took two days to get it from his hand into ours. The minute we got the name of the insurance company, we subpoenaed its records on the "theft."

While dictating the subpoena, I got the idea of also subpoenaing records of any other theft of papers that might have been claimed. It was a hunch that paid off. The 1964 work papers were nowhere mentioned on the list of stolen records in 1966, but even more significant was that the insurance company told us that in each and every year—1966, 1967, and 1968—Patrusky and Weinstein had reported records stolen, each time from the trunk of Weinstein's car! It reminded me of the old story: "I hear you had a big fire in your warehouse." "Shush—it's tomorrow."

Judge Wyatt excluded the testimony about the successive thefts, but when Patrusky left the stand this time, Allee didn't have the temerity to have our federal republic in all its majesty rerest. Instead, Perito mumbled something about the prosecution being finished. It was. Of course, accomplice witness Patrusky won't be prosecuted for perjury and blackmail, although I doubt that prospective clients will be breaking down his door. Reicher will not be prosecuted for extortion; his sentencing for his admitted perjury and grand larceny has been adjourned fourteen times. Weisman got formal immunity despite his admission that he bribed Reicher. So despite rejection of their testimony by the jury, the public is still picking up the tab of Morgenthau's feast. I was lucky in being able to give the lie to these accomplice witnesses. Others might not be. I shudder when I think of De-Sapio convicted by the word of an Itkin.

Indeed, the whole idea of accomplice witnesses leaves me uneasy. There are other ways to find the truth: undercover agents, who are much less likely to have motive for lying; disinterested fact witnesses; and documentary corroboration. But when it comes to our modern breed of accomplice witnesses, *caveat emptor.*

V

The Hanging Judge

JUDGES, OF COURSE, have the same biases, desires, and infirmities as other human beings. Many of them receive their judicial appointment through politics, through friendships with the right senator, or for whatever other reasons the facts of life might mandate. Many are great jurists and great human beings. Of the numerous examples available, one need only point to Chief Judge Stanley H. Fuld, of the New York Court of Appeals, or Phil Gibson, the retired chief justice of the California Supreme Court as models of competence, fairness, and courage.

On the other hand, there is a coterie of judges, known to the legal profession as hanging judges, who are consistently proprosecution and antidefendant. To ignore this fact is patently absurd. The danger to the impartial administration of justice is greatest in those jurisdictions where the prosecutor controls the assignment calendar and can in effect pick the judge before whom he wishes to try a case. As of the fall of 1970, assignments in New York Federal Court are being made by computer, which might be a way of eliminating this inequity.

Prosecutorial control can be done formally or informally, the practices differing in various jurisdictions. But often the prosecutor calls the turn one way or another. There are certain judges who don't automatically bow to the prosecution, however, and if you can get your client's case on the calendar when one of them is sitting, you have a fighting chance. In certain jurisdictions a defendant actually has an absolute right to challenge without reason a judge to whom his case is assigned. Illinois State Court is an example of a jurisdiction where the defendant is given one peremptory challenge of a judge.

With all the studies and criticisms of our system of justice, I have never quite understood how this system of prosecutors controlling assignments and picking convicting judges has escaped meaningful attention. When my alma mater, Columbia Law School, approached me to help finance a project about priority for negligence cases, I offered as a more worthy alternative to help finance a study of why convicting judges often end up with key cases.

First, the ground rules between a judge and the jury: The judge has the final say on the law, and the jury on the facts. In New York State a judge is not permitted to comment one way or another on the evidence. In federal court he is, but he must then instruct the jury that his comments are not binding on them and that they are the sole judges of the facts. While it is true that the right to comment on evidence is rarely exercised by federal judges, a judge can and does influence the outcome of a case over and above his rulings on the applicable law. He is often looked on with awe by the jury. He wears a black robe and sits on a raised platform next to the American flag. In some federal courts he is heralded each morning with "God Save These United States and This Honorable Court." His edge with the jury must often be substantial. And certain judges—the convicting ones—often abuse it. They have a thousand ways of communicating their bias to the jury. The way they treat counsel for either side, their treatment of witnesses, their facial expressions, the emphasis of words in their final charge to the jury—every lawyer must assess the power and influence on a jury of these factors. Let me offer some examples from my own experience.

Judge Herlands, who presided at the United Dye stock-swindle trial, was strictly a "convicting judge." A friend and client of ours was peripherally involved with Guterma as a glorified messenger boy when he was very young. As a result, he was named in a conspiracy indictment. He pleaded guilty to a misdemeanor and agreed to testify in the United Dye stock-swindle trial. A suspended sentence was promised to him by the prosecution. His lawyer, Tom Bolan, being very wise in the ways of men and judges, exacted one other commitment from the prosecution—that he be given a veto power over the judge before whom his client was to be sentenced. The client testified in the United Dye trial. Naturally, Judge Herlands praised his testimony as forthright, for he was a prosecution witness. But before time for his sentence came up, something new had been added—Morgenthau had become United States Attorney and was hell-bent on making a case against me. Our client was called down and asked to help. He explained that he could not truthfully say what they wanted him to. Suddenly his "sentencing" date was on the calendar, and at the prosecution's request the sentencing had been "referred to Judge Herlands." Quickly seeing the double cross that was under way, Tom moved to have the plea of guilty withdrawn. When that motion appeared on the calendar, the prosecutor advised the court that he had talked with Judge Herlands at home and that he had "consented" to have the motion referred to him. At the hearing before Herlands the prosecutor who agreed to give Bolan the veto power confirmed to Herlands that such an understanding had been reached. But Herlands nevertheless denied the motion, imposed a prison sentence, and then sadistically denied bail pending appeal. The higher court, however, promptly granted bail. Herlands was unmoved by the fact that the defendant's son was dying of leukemia and had only months to live. He would not defer the sentence.

I myself almost had to undergo one of Herland's mock trials. My first indictment was on September 3, 1963. Ordinarily, arraignment follows immediately. A prosecutor wants to keep things moving, particularly when Morgenthau is the prosecutor and I am the defendant. In my case, though, the arraignment was not scheduled until a much later date. Tom Bolan and I guessed immediately that a convicting judge must be sitting at that later date. We checked the calendar, and on the day Morgenthau scheduled, Judge Herlands was due to sit. We thwarted this maneuver by voluntarily walking in to plead ten days before the scheduled date. Over Morgenthau's objection a nonconvicting judge took my plea.

The incident was actually amusing. Judge Dudley Bonsal, who was presiding, asked the prosecutor why he objected to my pleading ahead of the day scheduled by the prosecutor. Morgenthau's assistant could not come out and tell the truth, which was that they wanted me to plead before Judge Herlands. Had that happened, I am certain that Judge Herlands, as a "great favor" to me as a professional man deserving an early trial, would have graciously consented to try the case himself—and I would have been writing this from Lewisburg Penitentiary. But Morgenthau's office could give no reason for delay, and my arraignment proceeded that day.

Our luck did not repeat at the second indictment—the one involving Weisman, Patrusky, and company. On preliminary matters I was before Federal Judges Bonsal, Edward Weinfeld, and Charles Metzner—each of whom was fair. Then in March, 1969, two months after the indictment, we ran into real difficulty. Our motions to dismiss the indictment were on the regular calendar, returnable March 25, 1969. But, as is not unusual, we could not meet the time schedule, largely because Morgenthau had suddenly abandoned an earlier S.E.C. indictment and switched over to the bribery-extortion case, which he felt was the stronger.

In November, 1968, Morgenthau had filed against me a ten-count indictment charging conspiracy and also a violation of S.E.C. laws, in that as counsel for some of the Krock and Muscat companies, we had prepared various formal filings with the Securities and Exchange Commission which allegedly "omitted" certain facts, thus making the filings incomplete. (This was about the best I could make out of it.) Just like the 1963 indictment, no accusations against me were made during the grand jury's entire eighteen-month term until the very last day, which was just a couple of weeks after Nixon became President-elect.

An unbroken tradition calls for replacement of appointive heads of administrative agencies, such as United States Attorneys like Morgenthau, when a new President of a different party from the previous one takes office. But trial of this indictment, which was handed up in November, 1968, was not pressed by Morgenthau, who decided to proceed instead with the Reicher one, which was not returned until January, 1969. I deem it inappropriate to comment here on the events and circumstances of this November, 1968, indictment because as of this writing, it remains unresolved.

We knew there was trouble as soon as we applied for a routine extension of the date to present our dismissal motions. When Tom Bolan and Myron Greene (the lawyer guiding the preliminaries) walked into the courtroom, they noted that Perito, the Morgenthau assistant who had done the talking on previous occasions, moved into the background, and another assistant, John Allee, took the floor. He demanded an early trial and seemed thoroughly confident. And with good reason. Judge Wyatt seemed completely hostile to us. His extension, so short that it was meaningless, was a Pyrrhic victory at best. And even though a different judge was due to sit on the new return date, he arranged to hear our motions himself. (In theory a judge does not hold on to motions that are adjourned beyond his term.) As to the trial, he said, "If the United States Attorney wants to try the case right away, I have to give great weight to it."

It turned out that the newly emerged prosecutor, Mr. Allee, had been associated in private practice with the judge's downtown law firm before the judge went on the bench. When Greene gave me this report, I smelled the whole picture. I told him that I would bet that Allee and the Morgenthau staff had in some way or another created an unfavorable impression of me in this judge's eyes and that the judge would follow up his act in holding on to the motions out of turn by trying to assign the actual trial of the case to himself. This was more of an empirical judgment than a prediction. I was hardly surprised later that month when I was called with the news that the judge had set the case for trial before none other than himself.

As I proceed to describe the events that transpired after Judge Wyatt entered my life, I wish to make it clear that in describing them I do not mean to characterize him as an example of a "hanging" judge. Although you will see that my experiences before him were less than comforting, it is only fair to say that many of his colleagues and members of the bar hold him in high esteem and do not label him as unfair at all. Indeed, a defendant with a prior record and an alleged "Mafia" taint, whom I successfully defended in a criminal case in July, 1970, was a great champion of Judge Wyatt, whom he felt had protected him against prosecutorial tyranny when the judge refused to comply with the district attorney's request that he be denied bail. It might just be that my own tribulations with Judge Wyatt were atypical and that he had been subconsciously preconditioned against me. And perhaps a strong element was his apparently unshakable belief in the integrity and high motive of all prosecutors, which resulted in his instinctively resenting the mere suggestion that what a prosecutor asked or did was not in good faith.

My forebodings as to my own situation took viable form as future events developed. As his new law clerk, the judge appointed Morgenthau's cousin, who had previously worked in the prosecutor's office for Morgenthau. The summer before the trial, Judge Wyatt went to Monte Carlo for his vacation. He is quite a Monte Carlophile. He also had an association with the Liberian Government. In his courthouse chamber suite the walls bear a large poster of the Monte Carlo Golf Club and a decoration from Liberia. It was coincidental that our firm was heavily involved with the Liberian Government at that time and for some years before. A client of ours had contracted with Liberia to build the multimillion-dollar Mt. Coffee Hydroelectric Power Project outside of Monrovia. After the contract was signed and work commenced, the United States Agency for International Development (AID) decided that it would put up the money instead. After all, just because private financing was available, why shouldn't they spend forty million dollars of United States taxpayers' money anyway? The only hitch was that our client had to agree to cancel his contract first. This was accomplished by giving him a state dinner, with fine liquor flowing, and presenting him with the same type of handsome decoration from the Liberian Government that I had seen on Judge Wyatt's wall. With the riband of the order draped across him and the little round boutonniere denoting his greatness placed in his lapel by President Tubman of Liberia, it was simple to add a fountain pen, with which our client proceeded to sign away all his rights, except for reimbursement. And when Judge Wyatt scheduled my case, we were in our fifth year of negotiating the amount of the reimbursement. As a matter of fact, the story dovetails even further. The eighteenth "final" settlement conference had been set for Monrovia in August, 1969. Our client had a summer home at Eden Roc on the French Riviera and summoned Tom Bolan and me to a strategy meeting there before leaving for Liberia. Tom went on to Monrovia, but I had to return home. Before doing so, I drove up to Monte Carlo to spend the weekend with another client.

At the Sporting Club at the beach in Monte Carlo everyone seems to know everyone else's business among the American summer colony. I greeted a number of old friends and spent the day around the beach. In the afternoon I went water-skiing. As I returned, a friend, Tom Corbally, was waiting for me out at the Point, where the ski boat docks. While I dried off, he gave me some almost unbelievable information: "The judge for your trial has been here having secret meetings with Perito, the prosecutor. You don't stand a chance." I knew that Wyatt did go to Monte Carlo, but I couldn't imagine the rest. I somehow didn't visualize Perito in Monte Carlo, and I certainly didn't conceive of Wyatt fraternizing with the prosecutor in my trial shortly before it was to begin. Tom went back to his source and returned with an insistence that it was Perito who had been with Wyatt. I repeated the story to Tom Bolan when he returned from Liberia.

Bolan thought we should not raise the point without concrete proof, because such conduct was a violation of the Canon of Judicial Ethics, which is designed to avoid even a suspicion of close association, either business or social, between either side and the judge at a forthcoming trial: "He [the judge] should, however, in pending or prospective litigation before him be particularly careful to avoid such action as may reasonably tend to awaken the suspicion that his social or business relations or friendships constitute an element in influencing his judicial conduct." If our information was inaccurate or if accurate but unprovable, the judge would have been even less inclined to control his bias.

But as it turned out, Wyatt himself confirmed that he had in fact entertained Morgenthau's assistant, Paul Perito, one of my prosecutors, at Monte Carlo. He stated:

> I invited Mr. Perito to use my tent at the beach. Thereafter, I think over a period of a week or ten days or something, I saw Mr. Perito from time to time and on one occasion—I believe just one—I took him to lunch.
>
> Now, I think if Mr. Perito had taken me to lunch and bought my lunch, however minor in degree, the proprieties might have been offended. But since I paid for Mr. Perito's lunch I don't think there is any question about it.

This hairline distinction as to who paid was of small comfort to me as I was about to go to trial before this judge.

This was the third such incident. Allee, the other of my prosecutors, had worked in Wyatt's law firm; the judge had appointed another Morgenthau assistant, who was also Morgenthau's cousin, as his law clerk; and now Perito had been Wyatt's guest shortly before the trial. But even more disconcerting was the way in which the judge managed to slip these ineluctable facts into the record as insignificant "by-the-way" disclosures.

The most puzzling example of Judge Wyatt's attitude came just before the trial when the judge, after having warned *Life* magazine of the consequences of publishing a pretrial smear against me, refused to give me any protection after its appearance. When we put in an affidavit outlining Morgenthau's collaboration with *Life* on the smear article, the judge didn't even require Morgenthau to file an answering one, nor did he. In the face of the mounting evidence of Judge Wyatt's hostility toward me, Tom Bolan consulted two eminent lawyers and two experienced judges. Three of the four counseled that we had no choice but to file a formal affidavit of prejudice against the judge, and ask him to have another judge try the case instead. The fourth predicted that Wyatt would never step aside—that he would only become that much more vindictive. The peculiar rule of law in this situation is that it is the judge accused of prejudice who determines himself whether he is prejudiced or not. It is really an absurd rule—like a defendant's being his own jury. An affidavit of prejudice is not a thing that can be done lightly. It must be sworn to not only by the alleged victim but also by his attorney. Under these circumstances one would think that such an application would be heard by another judge. It is hard to imagine a judge sustaining an affidavit and saying, "Yes, I'm prejudiced and you caught me at it." Judge Wyatt, of course, overruled our affidavit of prejudice and never seemed to forgive Tom Bolan for having certified it.

The judge frequently lost his cool during the trial and exploded in front of the jury, not only at my lawyer, Joe Brill, but at lawyers Dick Owen and Ed Garlock, who represented my codefendants. Both Owen and Garlock are perfect gentlemen in and out of a courtroom, and they were astonished at the judge's apparent hostility. Owen, who himself had served as an assistant United States Attorney under Judge J. Edward Lumbard, is very fair and very calm. But at one point while he was cross-examining Patrusky, eliciting information connected with the phony Exhibit X, the judge exploded at him so loudly that Owen literally fell back into his chair and couldn't continue his cross-examination.

Wyatt's prejudice was apparent to us from the preliminary stages of the trial. For instance, it is not at all unusual in highly controversial cases for the defense to suggest sequestering the jury (seeing that they're exposed to no outside publicity or contact). Because this is something of a hardship to the jury, to prevent possible prejudice the jury is not told which side requested the sequestration. Yet, to our surprise, the following exchange occurred:

BRILL: . . . I would respectfully ask your Honor effectively to sequester the jury from the possible taint of all of the news and publicity which attends this trial, and no matter how hard we try I don't think any of us are in the position to control the situation, and I did not see it myself, but I understand that both last night and this morning there was a very considerable amount of time devoted by the television channels to a discussion of this matter. The newspapers all carried accounts of it, and if we are to effectively try to control the prejudice which flows from the dissemination of publicity in the light of all that has transpired earlier, I think the jury must be entirely sequestered, and that is my application, and I would ask your Honor to sequester the jury, please.

THE COURT: Is it included in your application that I tell the jury that they are being sequestered at the request of the defendant?

BRILL: If your Honor did that I think it would be an inadvertent unfairness on your Honor's part. I don't think that the Court ever tells the jury that a particular party wants the jury sequestered. That obviously would prejudice that jury against that party and I don't think your Honor would want to do that.

THE COURT: I just wondered whether it was in contemplation in your motion that it would be explained to the jury that it had been on motion of the defendant, Mr. Cohn.

BRILL: I would be surprised if your Honor did that. It is not within the contemplation of my motion, your Honor. As a matter of fact, I think, as your Honor has raised the question, I would specifically ask your Honor not to say what the source of the application is because I think that would prejudice Mr. Cohn.

GARLOCK: I'm frank to say, your Honor, that if that were done I would request it as prejudicial error and request a mistrial.

Often we were not even able to question the credibility of major prosecution witnesses. Thus the judge would not permit us to question Patrusky about the tape recording in which he called Reicher a blackmailer who ought to be in jail. Nor were we allowed to offer proof that Reicher, who had denied having ever been arrested before, had been arrested for embezzlement.

When it came to Wyatt's rulings on our examination of witnesses, our whole case moved like lightning because as we called a witness to the stand, we would often be called to the side bar out of the hearing of the jury and made to give an off-the-record preview of what the witness was going to say. The judge would often summarily rule it out as irrelevant or as an improper something or other, and the witness would be off the stand before he started to testify. This is what happened to the witnesses on the Patrusky-Weinstein insurance "thefts." In fact, even the judge took cognizance of what he was doing. When Bolan said: "Your Honor, we have finished with these witnesses a lot faster than I thought we would," Judge Wyatt replied, "I suppose I had something to do with that."

When we first asked that Patrusky's work sheets remain in court overnight, Wyatt replied: "Now, wait. They are the property of the witness, and we'll have to arrange to have copies made of them unless the witness is willing to leave them here. What about that, Mr. Patrusky?"

But Joe Brill insisted: "Your Honor, I think they should be left with the clerk of the court in their original form." Most fortunately, as future events established, they were.

Wyatt even went so far as to suggest arguments for the prosecution to mitigate the effect of defense-witness testimony. Take the case of Burton Abrams, who acted as Weisman's attorney in 1964 when he sold his stock and left Fifth Avenue. Weisman's story was that he had been extorted into doing this by my threats that if he didn't sell out, I would go to city authorities and disclose his indiscretions with Reicher.

As further proof that my disclosure to Corporation Counsel Larkin came *before* the stock-sale negotiations began, Tom

Bolan and Joe Brill decided to interview Abrams before the trial. He said that when he was dealing with Weisman, both of them knew the disclosure had already been made.

At a discussion in Judge Wyatt's robing room one day— with the prosecution present—Wyatt suggested that Abrams almost had to say that the matter had been reported to the authorities, or Abrams himself might have been guilty of "misprision of a felony." This rarely used term means in effect that one who has knowledge of a felony and helps to conceal its disclosure might himself be guilty of suppressing the felony. Since the term is rare, we all remembered Wyatt's use of it and were surprised, since it did not fit the facts of our case.

The prosecution had their ears cocked, too. When Allee summed up to the jury, he made this very argument, actually using the term "misprision of felony."

Now confronted with the judge's theory actually turning up in the prosecution's summation, we decided to make a record of the matter. We started plowing through the transcript to find the passage where Wyatt had used the controversial term. He found the passage, but the term wasn't there. Garlock called us over and we all looked. The term "misprision of felony" as used by Wyatt did not appear in the official transcript.

We followed an angry Ed Garlock into the judge's robing room. After establishing by everyone's recollection that the term had been used but not recorded, the following colloquy ensued:

> GARLOCK: Your Honor, the term "misprision of a felony" has not passed through my unconscious mind since I was a law-school student. I don't think I heard anybody use the term since I got out of law school, and it made a striking impression on me at the time, partly because of its relative strangeness to my ears and partly because I was shocked by

your Honor's suggestion of that possibility in relation to Mr. Abrams. So that recollection is vivid.

THE COURT: Well, I am prepared to accept your recollection.

BOLAN: I will say, your Honor, that I remember that very clearly, that that expression was used.

THE COURT: Well, I will accept that. But what follows from it?

GARLOCK: Well, as I say, your Honor, it suggests to me and it merely reinforces an impression I previously had that your Honor has, as I said before, been astute on behalf of the Government and somewhat less than astute when it comes to the protection of the defendants' rights. I think, with all due respect, sir, that the record will bear me out. In any case, that is the purpose of my putting it in the record.

Perhaps his most devastating thrusts at us were his handling of matters before the jury. Anything that might work to our advantage was discussed in private. Although he conceded on the record in his anteroom that there was no evidence against me on the two most serious counts in the indictment, those dealing with the Reicher bribe, he nevertheless submitted them to the jury:

BOLAN: . . . So where is there any evidence that Mr. Cohn, prior to February 6th, or whatever date it is, promised to pay Mr. Reicher any money?

THE COURT: I don't think there is any such evidence.

BOLAN: Well, I submit that it shouldn't go to the jury.

THE COURT: I am giving a charge which may be too favorable to Mr. Cohn, but I am charging that any payment to Reicher after February 6, 1964—that they would have to find that it was made pursuant to an agreement known to Mr. Cohn. If it was known to Mr. Cohn, then I think that is sufficient.

At the end of the trial, Judge Wyatt did something I believe to be without precedent. In his charge the judge customarily instructs the jury as to the law, which is his area, mentioning the facts only as necessary to guide the jury in applying the law. In our case Wyatt advised that he, too, was going into the facts in his charge in some detail by "marshaling" the evidence. All defense counsel objected, but Wyatt wouldn't budge. Then came the crusher: In his marshaling of the evidence to the jury he would summarize only the direct testimony of government witnesses, without specific reference to the facts brought out on their cross-examination. So that if Weisman said on direct that he was extorted into selling the stock, but on cross changed his testimony and admitted the real reasons, the jury would be reminded by the judge only of the extortion charge.

As I said to the judge in the anteroom: "Mr. Allee is going to be the last one to sum up to the jury, your Honor. I don't think he needs the Court's help, too—maybe he does, but I don't think he is entitled to get it." But as we listened to the judge's "marshaling" the evidence, we thought the prosecution did get help.

Some of the Court's comments during the summations themselves were far from comforting. There was the end of Garlock's summation, when his traditional laudatory comments about me were harshly interrupted by the Court:

> GARLOCK: I have just a few parting comments in farewell to say.
>
> First a few words about Mr. Cohn, and I can say them because to some degree Mr. Kiser's fate is bound up—certainly not exclusively—with Mr. Cohn's here.
>
> Mr. Cohn is a well-known controversial public figure. That is apparent to all of us. If you didn't know it independently, the injunctions and admonitions of the Court not to read in the press and not to listen on the radio about this case would suggest to you that he is a person—
>
> ALLEE: I have to object to this, your Honor.
>
> THE COURT: Yes, of course, Mr. Garlock, as I told the jury repeatedly, we are here to try the issues framed by the indictment, that and that alone.

GARLOCK: Actually that was merely introductory to something that is relevant—

THE COURT: It is not a proper comment.

GARLOCK: The record here shows that quite without any direct character witnesses as to the high standing of Mr. Cohn in the community, I think you are entitled to take that into consideration.

ALLEE: I have to object to this, your Honor.

THE COURT: Yes, that has nothing to do with the matter at all. There is no such evidence in the record.

GARLOCK: I beg your pardon, sir?

THE COURT: I say there is no such evidence in the record. Let's go on, Mr. Garlock, please.

GARLOCK: Your Honor, there is reference—

THE COURT: There is no evidence of it, whatever it may mean —and I will instruct the jury on that—there is no evidence about reputation for honesty, truth, and veracity.

GARLOCK: I am talking about his standing—

THE COURT: Well, anything else is wholly immaterial—wholly immaterial.

GARLOCK: I think inference can be drawn from certain aspects of the record. But I will pass it.

Later, in the robing room, Tom Bolan challenged Judge Wyatt's handling of this situation in the presence of the jury:

BOLAN: . . . When Mr. Garlock was summing up he was endeavoring to make a statement about Mr. Cohn's standing in the community, or what have you.

We didn't request that statement.

Your Honor interrupted Mr. Garlock with a statement that was wholly uncalled for, I submit. To say there is nothing in the record as to Mr. Cohn's reputation for truth, honesty, and integrity is a highly prejudicial remark, and wholly uncalled for on Mr. Garlock's statement.

I understand from Mr. Garlock that he was simply going to refer to statements in the record elicited by the government on cross-examination, statements as to positions held

by Mr. Cohn, et cetera, for which he had a perfect right
to comment. And then your Honor makes this statement to
the jury that there is nothing in the record as to Mr. Cohn's
reputation for truth, honesty, and veracity, and your Honor
made that statement after Mr. Garlock mentioned something about the fact that there were no character witnesses.
   It just highlighted, your Honor, that situation.

THE COURT: Mr. Garlock's remark was wholly improper and
   should never have been heard and made and needed to be
   corrected, and I did correct it.

BOLAN: You mean, your Honor, that Mr. Garlock, for example, could not point out that there was testimony without
   objection that Mr. Cohn was the president of a particular
   organization?

GARLOCK: Or a regent of a college? That is in the record, your
   Honor. Or that he was retained by Cardinal Spellman in the
   school-prayer case?

BOLAN: I point out again that what your Honor, I submit,
   should have done if he felt that Mr. Garlock's remarks were
   improper was to call a side-bar conference or to request him
   to proceed on to another subject, rather than to say that to
   the jury: "There is nothing in the record as to Mr. Cohn's
   reputation for honesty and integrity."

Another incident that shocked many observers occurred
when Tom Bolan tried to stop Allee from making the patent
misstatement that it had been the prosecution and not the
defense that had requested the recall of Patrusky after the
defense's announcement that it was having Exhibit X examined for authenticity produced Patrusky's confession that
it was a phony.

The incident arose when Allee was trying to convince the
jury about the fair manner in which Morgenthau's prosecution of me had been conducted. As he opened his summation, he accused the defense of seeking "to divert your
attention from the issues in this case by irresponsibly attack-

ing the motives and the conduct and the integrity of the
prosecutors representing the United States of America."

Allee then proceeded to give this account of phony Exhibit X and Patrusky's recall to the stand: "Indeed, ladies
and gentlemen, I think you may find on the record in this
case that we not only did not do these terrible things but
that we bent over backward to insure the accuracy of the
evidence that came before you, and I'm referring in that
connection to our immediately recalling Mr. Patrusky to the
stand. . . ."

This blatant misrepresentation brought Tom to his feet,
and his exchange with Wyatt in the presence of the jury
follows:

> BOLAN: I object, your Honor. He was recalled at our request.
> THE COURT: I will not permit that.
> BOLAN: That is a fact.
> THE COURT: The government brought this matter to my atten-
> tion first. You had nothing whatever to do with it.
> BOLAN: I beg your Honor's pardon. I requested Mr. Patrusky
> —it was our request. The record—
> THE COURT: Sir, will you take your seat.
> BOLAN: May I just say—
> THE COURT: Your interruption is wholly—
> BOLAN: They brought the matter to our attention. We re-
> quested—
> THE COURT: Will you listen to me?
> BOLAN: Yes.
> THE COURT: Your interruption is wholly uncalled for. You
> keep your seat until you have something worthy to rise for.
> [*The New York Times* reports that before saying this,
> "Judge Wyatt rose from his red leather chair in visible an-
> ger and banged his gavel."] Proceed, Mr. Allee.
> ALLEE: Thank you, sir.

Bolan brought the actual transcript into the judge's robing room to show he had been mistaken in what he had said in the course of his explosion at Tom in front of the jury:

BOLAN: Your Honor, I have an application concerning what I deem to be highly prejudicial remarks made by your Honor in the presence of the jury today and yesterday during the summation.

Now today I refer to the statement concerning Mr. Patrusky.

The record clearly shows that on November 21, 1969, at page 5,172, after the Government disclosed the information about the time the document, Exhibit X, was prepared, that the Government said that it had two suggestions, two proposals, and Mr. Allee stated as follows: "And unless there is some objection from the defendants the Government would propose one of two courses. One would be to reopen the record, reopen the Government's case and all allow us to call Mr. Weinstein." The second proposal was: "or that the Court call Mr. Weinstein as the Court's witness since we have now closed."

Mr. Allee said there was a problem, however, that Mr. Weinstein has had a heart attack and that he would at least like to consult with his . . . doctor before he actually goes to the stand.

. . .

Now on page 7,178 your Honor said to Mr. Allee: "Mr. Allee, do you have in mind doing anything else than putting Weinstein on the stand?"

ALLEE: *That is all, your Honor* [italics mine]. I've got a problem on that now. I have a report that the doctor says under no circumstances could he allow his patient to go on the stand in a public courtroom.

Then *Mr. Brill* [italics mine] says: "Well, this may necessitate a change in the request that we were going to put to your Honor. We thought that both Messrs. Patrusky and Weinstein should be available Monday morning."

. . .

Your Honor, I point out at no point was there any suggestion that the Government was going to call Mr. Patrusky back. It was only when Mr. Brill said, "We want Patrusky here to cross-examine him" that your Honor then said, "Well, that is all right, but if the Government wants to examine first, all right."

.   .   .

The Government didn't come in and say: "We want to reopen to put Mr. Weinstein and Mr. Patrusky on."

No, sir. They said Weinstein. The logical one for them to call was Patrusky. He is the man who gave the testimony, not Weinstein, but they came in offering to put a man on that they knew had a bad heart attack and that there was doubt as to whether he would testify, so for Mr. Allee—

THE COURT: Why do you say that they knew he had a bad heart attack?

BOLAN: They said they were told he had.

THE COURT: They had not had any doctor's report at that time.

BOLAN: I am just reporting what Mr. Allee said. Mr. Allee said that when he came in—

THE COURT: They didn't know how I would rule on the availability of Weinstein. I didn't know how I would rule on the availability of Weinstein.

BOLAN: They had their common sense and we have it as lawyers. Mr. Patrusky was the one who testified—

THE COURT: No, but you are attempting now in your remarks, in open court you are attempting to suggest in some way that the defendants, because they asked for Patrusky, had discovered something.

BOLAN: No.

THE COURT: They didn't discover anything. It was the Government that brought it to my attention.

BOLAN: Your Honor, of course it came in after we said that we are going to age the documents, that Mr. Patrusky came in. I made no insinuation that it wasn't called to our attention. It is very clear in the record, your Honor, how it happened that Mr. Patrusky came and told the Government, and the Government—that is not the point. The point is—

THE COURT: And the Government came promptly to me.

BOLAN: Yes, they came promptly to your Honor, yes, but not with any request that Mr. Patrusky be called. We as lawyers, you as a judge, would know, and I think we do, that the logical thing would be to put Mr. Patrusky back.

THE COURT: Certainly not. The logical thing would be to put the man in whose handwriting the document is in.

BOLAN: No, your Honor, the—

THE COURT: Of course, it would be.

BOLAN: The logical thing was to explain Mr. Patrusky's—what he based his testimony on. He based it on what Mr. Weinstein told him. That is the only way you could rehabilitate Mr. Patrusky, show how he was mistaken, not to bring in some third party without even the intermediate step of having Mr. Patrusky explain how, when he said it was written five years ago, that he based it on what Mr. Weinstein told him. That is what you do logically. They did not ask that he be recalled.

In his charge to the jury the judge actually suggested that they disbelieve one of our key witnesses. This incident centered on the days in January, 1964, when Steinreich and I were worried about the possibility of a mistrial in the condemnation case if Reicher, the city appraiser, testified as a witness for the city, and it came to light later that he had had surreptitious dealings with company officials. Our objective was to get this initially to the attention of Fifth's board and its senior trial counsel in the condemnation case. We knew that Weisman would not voluntarily call a meeting for this purpose, since he would be exposing himself. Fifth's bylaws provided that any four directors could bring about a board meeting by formal demand. On January 17, 1964, four of them did so in a telegram, setting the meeting for January 20, 1964. A defense witness, Solomon Silbert, who was one of the directors of the company at the time, testified

to having received such a telegram and having gone to the
meeting on January 20, only to find some directors present,
others absent, and a general state of confusion. In his charge
to the jury Judge Wyatt took the almost unprecedented step
of suggesting that the jury disbelieve Silbert's testimony on
the grounds that Silbert could not have received the January
17 telegram from the four directors, since it had been sent
only to Weisman as president of the company and, further,
that no such meeting occurred:

> In considering this matter about the request for a special meet-
> ing and Silbert's testimony, the jury may consider whether or
> not a meeting for January 20, 1964, was called. The jury may
> consider that the telegram sent by the four directors to Weis-
> man is not itself the call of a meeting, which it would be nat-
> ural to send to all directors, but on the contrary is a request
> that Weisman—as chairman of the board and president of
> Fifth—himself call a special meeting of the board. The jury
> may consider whether any reason is suggested why such a
> telegram should be sent to Silbert or any other director, who so
> far as appears had no authority to call any meeting of the
> board.

This charge, even if true, was an unwarranted interference with the jury's province. But what the judge told the
jury was totally inaccurate factually. The truth was that
right on the face of the January 17, 1964, telegram (a
prosecution exhibit) was the message "A copy of this telegram is being sent to each director of the company." And
the witness who confirmed that there had been a meeting
and Silbert's account of it was the prosecution's principal
witness—Larry Weisman himself!

Thus, the prosecution's key witness had himself confirmed
the testimony of Silbert, which Wyatt implied to the jury
was untruthful. When confronted, Wyatt's only extenuation
was to suddenly declare that certain questions put to Weis-

man two months earlier had been "improper" and that he must have been asleep when they were asked!

Tom Bolan was loaded for bear. As soon as the charge was over, he went into the judge's robing room and made his point, following which Judge Wyatt agreed to go back in and read the telegram to the jury. But the matter became academic by that evening, when the jury filed in and acquitted me.

At no time during any of these exchanges did anyone connected with the defense treat the judge with anything but complete courtesy. The strongest response during the whole trial was Bolan's in the matter of the January, 1964, telegram, and that was in the robing room out of the presence of the jury.

A sad example of judicial vindictiveness comes from Federal Judge Robert Shaw in New Jersey. After a long investigation, former Jersey City Mayor John V. Kenny was indicted in November, 1970. Mayor Kenny is seventy-seven years old and has been in poor health. He has not been tried and is clothed with a presumption of innocence. His family ties and roots are all in New Jersey, and I doubt that there is a person around who thinks that the elderly gentleman is going to jump bail. But Judge Shaw actually denied Kenny permission to go to Florida. Unreasoning judicial meanness of this caliber gives lawyers the creeps.

Lawyers should be as familiar with the predilections and track record of the judge they are appearing before as they are with applicable case law. Some law professors teach on the assumption that all judges think and rule alike. This is so far from the truth that probably no element in a criminal case is more important than securing a fair and impartial presiding judge.

VI

"His Own Lawyer"

"A MAN WHO'S HIS own lawyer has a fool for a client" is an admonitory clause that has been used to threaten just about every lawyer who ever thought of representing himself. When I was under fire at the nationally televised Army-McCarthy hearings in 1954, I testified once briefly and later in the hearings at length on all the issues. My initial brief appearance was disastrous, and I was cut up by that wily old fox who was the army's counsel, the late Joseph Welch, of Boston. This poor performance of mine touched off a demand by my friends that I be represented by outside counsel when testifying fully in my own defense. After much thought I rejected the advice and decided to learn from my earlier mistakes. I continued to appear without counsel, and it went quite satisfactorily. I had no further problems as I faced questioning by Welch, Committee Counsel Ray Jenkins, and the seven senators on the committee. I was able to keep my cool, and Mr. Welch's vigorous attempts to bait me into losing it under cross-examination caused a sharp reaction against the army's side.

Possibly as a result of this experience, from the time of my first indictment in 1963, I had a half-conscious desire to be my own lawyer. Everyone whose advice I valued was horrified at the idea. The old saying was thrown at me frequently and emphatically. I realized the difference between my role at the Army-McCarthy hearings and as a defendant in a criminal trial, and I saw the drawbacks of the idea. For example, the awkwardness of cross-examining a witness against me who was or had been a friend of mine could only result in his saying to me, "Roy, you know you told me that," etc. Further, if it became necessary to argue with the judge or a witness in front of the jury, I would be presenting the wrong "image" for my cause. In the course of the summation I could hardly praise myself for any conceivable virtues. And deep down, I felt unequal to the task. I knew that Clarence Darrow had defended himself. I also knew that I wasn't Clarence Darrow.

In fact, I had never defended anyone in a criminal case, and I realized there were many in the field who had forgotten more than I would ever know. So I finally decided to eliminate myself as a candidate, and Tom and I began the search for defense counsel. From an image standpoint the best choice would have been a highly prestigious, slightly stuffy Wall Street lawyer, to contrast with my relative youth and well-advertised brashness. I knew several of the logical choices very well. But I knew that because of my controversiality, they would duck it. They did. After protestations of their desire to help me, they would regretfully conclude that an undefined "conflict of interest" or prior commitment made the realization of their good intention impossible. I noted with some amusement that one firm that turned me down subsequently willingly appeared for Rev. William Sloane Coffin, of Yale, to defend him against charges of having encouraged the burning of draft cards.

Then, one afternoon, my falling spirits were revived by words spoken to me from across the desk in a skyscraper office at One Chase Manhattan Plaza in the heart of Wall Street.

"I knew your father, I have observed you as my adversary in a hotly contested civil suit. I have followed your indictment, and I believe you are innocent. If you wish, I should be pleased to represent you, and there will be no fee." The offices were those of one of the largest and most prestigious law firms in the United States—Davis, Polk, Wardwell, Sunderland & Kiendl. The man speaking was its senior partner, Theodore Kiendl. In his seventies and with Parkinson's disease he remained the dean of the American bar. His ability and courtroom presence had won for him the reputation as perhaps the country's leading trial lawyer. He was representing a lawyer in a malpractice suit brought by one of my clients, and that is how I had met him. I immediately and gratefully accepted his offer. He explained that he would have to obtain the permission of his client, who was being sued by my client, and notify his partners at Davis, Polk. We both thought this a formality and foresaw no problems, but he phoned me the next day to say that while his client had given permission, one of his law partners, Hazard Gillespie, said it would be impossible for Kiendl to represent me. Kiendl continued: "The mystifying part is that Hazard won't tell me why—but keeps saying that while he cannot disclose why now, the reason will become clear to both of us shortly." And of course it did, just before the trial, when our lawyer received a message from Gillespie that he had vital information bearing on the case and wished to be called as a defense witness.

Mr. Kiendl's offer to represent me for nothing was most generous, since the usual fee for such a trial runs in the vicinity of fifty thousand dollars and over.

The lawyer whom Tom and I selected was not from New York City. He was Frank G. Raichle, the eloquent and affable leader of the bar in Buffalo, who had served as president of the American College of Trial Lawyers. Raichle is typical of the breed of great trial lawyers—all instinct, courtroom presence, and little need for preparation. This was fortunate, as we had no time for preparation. The case went to trial within a few weeks of our having retained Raichle. Tom and I followed him to Miami where the American College was meeting, and we managed to sneak in a few hours' work a day.

Raichle's genius is his distinguished courtroom presence and his keen sense of both drama and humor. He had a winning smile, a twinkle in his eye, and always the last word. For instance, he was cross-examining a lawyer named George Rosier who Swann claimed was with him the same afternoon I placed my meeting with Garfield, Swann, and Gottesman. The exact hours were important. In the course of Raichle's examination it developed that the lawyer had supposedly had lunch with Swann, let Swann pay the check, and also charged Swann for the time. To relieve Rosier's discomfort, the judge leaned down and said to Raichle: "Now, Mr. Raichle, I'll bet you've done the same thing yourself!" The courtroom now laughed at Raichle's expense. But Raichle broke into a grin and replied, "Of course, your Honor, how do you think I knew what question to ask?"

When another witness under stiff cross-examination exasperatedly shouted, "I'm trying to tell the truth!" Raichle shot back, "You're not doing a very good job of it, are you?"

And when Swann himself finally slinked off the stand with his past fraudulent activities and his present lies exposed, he was so relieved that he eagerly asked the judge: "Am I excused?"

> THE COURT: You are excused.
> SWANN: To go home?
> THE COURT: To go home.

As Swann hurtled for the exit door, Raichle shook his finger at him and added, "Be good."

Another example, after Raichle had caught Garfield in serious contradictions:

RAICHLE: You are under oath, my good man. Did—
GARFIELD: I—
ASSISTANT U.S. ATTORNEY WALPIN: Objection.
RAICHLE: You object to my calling him a good man?
THE COURT: Wait a minute, wait a minute.

When it came to the 1969 trial, all of the same problems on counsel selection reappeared. Raichle was tied up in Buffalo trying a case for Cornell University. I thought of myself again, and again realized it would be unwise. Myron Greene, one of the community's most able and respected lawyers, agreed to handle at least the preliminary stages and refused to accept any compensation for it.

When personal reasons made it necessary for Mike Greene to withdraw from the trial itself, Tom and I figured (correctly) that Judge Wyatt wouldn't give us a one-second adjournment. Veteran trial lawyer Joe Brill agreed to handle the case—he had a complete dedication to my innocence and was outraged at the charges—and was willing to get ready in a short time. But the judge would not even give him that. So Tom and I handled the jury selection. Joe's appearance is striking. He has a bald head and a heavy beard and moustache, and he also possesses an incisive mind and a dogged ability at cross-examination.

When there is a conspiracy case and more than one defendant is on trial, teamwork among defense counsel is a great asset, and dissension among them can be a disaster. I was always very fortunate in this respect. Henry Chapman, Murray Gottesman's lawyer in the first trial, worked very well with Raichle, and the jury obviously enjoyed Chapman's persistence and sincerity. Brill worked equally well with the lawyers for my two codefendants—Dick Owen and Ed Garlock. Owen had served in the United States Attorney's office with Tom Bolan. He has an intense sincerity and a pleasant manner. Ed Garlock is a man of deep feeling and great eloquence.

Brill, Owen, and Garlock would make the decisions jointly. There was no dissension. A contrast was in the De-Sapio trial. His codefendant's lawyer was at sword's point with DeSapio's lawyer right in front of the jury all through the trial. It was disastrous.

Joe Brill's cross-examination of the prosecution witnesses was masterful. Many seasoned courtroom observers felt that he had so totally demolished Morgenthau's case that we could have rested without offering any defense of our own. His style is different from Raichle's. Brill sticks right to the questions at hand and does not interject any humor into the proceedings. He is persistent and relentless. One could sense that the jury admired him. And he never lost his temper at the judge's unfairness. His strongest response would be: "I'm sorry I must disagree with your Honor." But the tongue-lashings he received from Judge Wyatt took their toll.

"Why must he think he knows everything and ridicule every defense contention?" Brill would comment in the car after court. "Instead of just ruling on the law, he always has to question the good faith of any position we assert. His favorite words are 'bad faith,' 'frivolous,' and 'pettifogging.'"

The climax came over the Morgenthau "vendetta" issue. The judge decided well before the trial that my game was to "try" Morgenthau instead of being tried myself. He was quite wrong. Even if it had been permissible, I was not about to detract from the good case I knew we had by risking the possibility that Morgenthau had an admirer or two on the jury. But the "vendetta" business had to come in on one issue—the "deals" made by prosecution witnesses with Morgenthau to save their own necks at my expense. This point was clearly relevant on the question of the prosecution's witnesses' motives for testifying against me. The judge agreed that this was the law, and questions on this subject were proper, but when Brill pursued them, he would cut him off.

At one point, he threatened to hold Mr. Brill in contempt of court. Mr. Brill, who has an impeccable record after forty years of practice and the respect of the bench and bar, was horrified. After the account of this tirade hit the press, Brill's sixteen-year-old son told his father, "Dad, don't worry. Even the very liberal kids at school who were rapping me because you're defending Roy Cohn are all for you after the way the press reports the judge is pushing you around."

On the morning of the last day of the cross-examination of the prosecution's last witness, Bernard Patrusky, the judge issued his customary blast at Mr. Brill.

At noon, as we walked over to Gasner's for lunch, Joe said to Tom Bolan and me: "I don't know why I let him get under my skin. I receive fair and courteous treatment from so many of the judges down here—I guess I keep expecting it here and forget that this man thinks he is on a crusade against you." Lunch at Gasner's over, he said he was still upset and wanted to walk back slowly alone, and he left us to return to the courtroom. When Tom and I arrived there, Mr. Brill was slumped down in his leather chair in the almost empty courtroom with severe chest pains. He was taken on a stretcher to the courthouse's first-aid room. I rushed to the phone and called Joe's secretary, who contacted his personal physician, Dr. Bianco, who rushed over. Dr. Bianco examined Mr. Brill, then telephoned the hospital for an ambulance. Mr. Brill had had a serious heart attack. He was to suffer two more, and five months later he had still not returned to work. (Significantly, Judge Wyatt never once inquired about Mr. Brill's health or progress.)

At this time, the prosecution had just rested. The defense was about to begin. There had been some speculation as to whether or not I would take the stand. In a criminal trial a defendant may testify, but need not. If he doesn't, the law is that his failure to do so may not be considered against him in any way. Occasionally—and maybe frequently —despite this legal doctrine, jurors are adversely influenced by a defendant's failure to take the stand on the theory that he must be hiding something. I felt that the possibility of such an inference was even stronger in the case of someone as well known as I am, and I had decided to take the stand. We had spent many hours preparing an outline of my testimony. Cross-examination did not worry me, since I would be telling the truth and had sufficient background not to be trapped.

But Mr. Brill's heart attack changed our strategy. We had two voids to fill: presentation of our witnesses on our direct case and the summation to the jury. Tom and I agreed that if I testified, I should not sum up, and that if I summed up, I should not testify. Filling both roles would be too much of me in a short span. The Court had been told by the prosecution at the outset that he case would run about three weeks. But the "three-week" case had already lasted nearly two months. The Christmas holidays were almost upon us. The jurors, with good reason, were becoming impatient. If I were on the stand for days and then summed up, they might justifiably be ready to lynch me. Tom had missed part of the trial because of the successive deaths of two members of his family, and he was therefore concerned about his summing up. He said he had more than he could handle in taking over at the last minute the preparation of our ten to fifteen witnesses and examining them at the trial.

Mr. Brill, whom we saw in the hospital the next day, was emphatic—I should sum up in my own behalf. I agreed, and this decision having been reached, it followed that I would not also testify and that Tom would present our witnesses. We decided to keep this strategy a secret.

I have heard it implied that our course of action was all prearranged and that Mr. Brill's illness was synthetic. Of course, neither of these charges was true.

The night after Mr. Brill's attack, when I knew I was to sum up, I dictated a draft to our secretary, Ann Turchiano, just to get some ideas down on paper. The first draft was forty-three pages. I set out to shorten it, but the second was over sixty pages. I knew the facts of the case, but what bothered me was the lack of a start and a finish. I just couldn't find thoughts for the opening and closing with which I would be comfortable. The problem about a start was solved the night before I summed up.

While I was grabbing a bite to eat in the kitchen, the phone rang. I told one of the boys working with me to tell whoever it was that I'd call back—I was too tired to walk ten steps to the phone. He returned and said, "It's Frank Raichle from Buffalo, with an idea." I knew enough about the quality of Frank's ideas to gain the strength to get to the phone. He said, typically, "I have a thought for your opening line. It's just a thought, and don't feel obligated to use it. It's probably no good." I already had a pad and pen in my hand. When I rose to face the jury, the words were basically Frank's: "This is the first time in my life I have ever addressed a jury in a criminal case. When I was back in law school, little did I dream that my first time would be in my own behalf."

The finish was the work of the Almighty, Judge Wyatt, and me—in that order. It came to me later that same night.

During delays due to illness of counsel, parties, and jurors, the judge got into the habit of leaving the jury with a sermonette. One day it came from Ecclesiastes: "Better it is the end of a thing than the beginning thereof." This kept going through my mind as I thought out my summation. I thought of Weisman, the prosecution's first witness, as the beginning of Morgenthau's case, and Patrusky, the last witness, as the end. I thought of the fiction in the grandiose beginning of the indictment, "The grand jury charges," and of the official title of the case, "The United States of America against Roy M. Cohn." I thought of what the judge would do to me if we lost. The probable sentence from most judges would have ranged from a fine to two years' imprisonment. Tom Bolan and I made an educated guess after the trial that Wyatt would have given me five years. I also thought of the jury standing between me and Morgenthau and the judge. As it all came together in my mind, I wrote down in longhand draft the words that would be the conclusion of my summation, and I never changed them.

The fact that I was to sum up was a relatively well guarded secret. We told no one in advance. Our turn to sum up was due for Tuesday morning, December 9, but the lawyers for my codefendants ran over, and after a brilliant job, finished at 3:35 in the afternoon. Less than an hour was left before court adjourned for the day. The judge leaned down toward Tom Bolan and said, "Mr. Bolan, would you care to address the jury now?"

I was amused at the judge's constant use of the phrase "address the jury," instead of the standard "sum up." It made the whole thing sound like a banquet with after-dinner speeches. We had known this moment would come and had discussed how to handle it. The possibilities were: (1) I just get up and start summing up. (2) We tell the judge privately that I was going to sum up. (3) Tom stand up and make a short explanation in open court. We hadn't resolved the matter until the lunch recess that day, when we were joined at Gasner's by Myron Greene, his highly capable associate, Howard Udell, and Frank Raichle. We talked it out.

We immediately rejected the second alternative, which might have led to my being given all sorts of admonitions as to what I could say and how I should say it. We rejected the first as too abrupt a transition. This left the third.

Tom Bolan rose at the counsel table. As he started to

speak, it became obvious that he was not summing up but was making some kind of a statement instead. The prosecution lawyers, Allee and Perito, looked bewildered and unsure of what, if anything, to do. The judge was momentarily speechless. Tom said: "Your Honor, because of the death of my younger brother at the beginning of this trial, I missed a week of trial testimony, and then, three weeks later, I had another death in the family and was off the case for a while.

"And when Mr. Brill was stricken with a heart attack, I was instructed——"

Allee broke in: "Could we have this at the side bar?"

Tom is a first-rate debater and public speaker. He has a ringing voice, and when he is interrupted against his wishes, his voice automatically becomes stronger and drowns out the interruptor. Although the transcript carries Allee's words, not many people heard them. Tom, in a louder voice, continued: "This will take just a minute. I am going to say that because of Mr. Brill's heart attack, I was instructed to go on. I told Mr. Cohn that I would do my best to prepare the defense and the witnesses but that Mr. Cohn would have to prepare for the summation.

"Mr. Cohn has done that, and Mr. Cohn is now ready to sum up on his own behalf."

Before I realized it, I was standing in front of the jury box facing the jurors. Out of the corner of my eye I saw the press dashing out the door. I did have a sense of the significance of the moment for my whole future. I am told my voice was low and unsure as I recited the opening lines:

May it please the Court. Mr. Foreman, ladies and gentlemen of the jury.

This is the first time in my life I have ever addressed a jury in behalf of a defendant in a criminal case. When I went to law school, little did I dream that my first time in this role would be in my own behalf.

What I was to say next had occurred to me only within the past half hour and was not known even to Tom. When Ed Garlock, who had preceded me, threw in a few kind words about my standing in the community, Allee objected, and the judge emphatically sustained his objection. With this incident fresh in everyone's mind I tried to use it to my advantage. Directly after my opening lines, I turned to the judge.

> I want to say at the outset in light of the colloquy between Mr. Allee and his Honor and Mr. Garlock a few moments ago, that of course I subscribe to exactly what his Honor said: The only thing we have before us here are the issues in this indictment. If I have done anything good in my life, I expect no credit for it in this case. Nor do I expect to be blamed here for any past position I've taken with which you might not agree.
>
> We are here to try the issues in this case, and my address to you will concern only the issues in this case.

I felt that in this way I was able to politely point up the judge's hostility toward me—having tried to damage me for something I had not even said or known Mr. Garlock was going to say. Later, I stuck to this same theme and "agreed" with the judge that Morgenthau's feud with me had no bearing on this case.

The second confrontation between the judge and me came only minutes later, when I said, "Now, if I have to say something about the law here in discussing the facts, anything I do say is, of course, subject to what his Honor tells you in his charge."

> THE COURT: I would say, Mr. Cohn, as little as possible about the law. I am going to instruct the jury fully on the law, and if were you, I would stick closely to the facts. . . .

COHN: . . . Believe me, your Honor, I have enough to do, and I
certainly don't want to indulge in your province and go into
the law too much at all.

I used his interruption to emphasize to the jury that they,
and not he, were the determiners of the facts. Turning again
to the jury, I continued: "Just as his Honor is the final judge
of the law, you and you alone are the final judges of the
facts under the system under which we operate in this country."

When I turned to the facts in the case, I had a decision to
make. The logical order would have been to start with the
first count, conspiring to bribe Reicher, and proceed chrono-
logically by count. "Don't do it that way," Tom Bolan had
advised me the night before. "Skip Count One. Its compli-
cated and boring. Go right to Counts Two and Three, about
the Patrusky payments. While those are most damaging, the
testimony is most incredible. Start with Patrusky and destroy him. Then go back to Count One."

As I spoke, I still wasn't sure which of the two courses I
would follow. I now looked at all the jurors closely. The reaction was encouraging. They seemed most attentive and recep-
tive. The women particularly looked kind. I decided to follow
Tom's advice. I skipped the first count and turned immediately to the Patrusky story. I went directly to the most damaging part—the two counts alleging that I had given money
to Patrusky for Reicher. I began to enjoy myself as I showed
how neither could have occurred, how Patrusky lied about a
conversation concerning a ticket agency I hadn't yet purchased, about an employee I hadn't yet hired, about a witness he "saw" on the stand who wasn't.

Indeed, I pointed out not only Patrusky's lie about having
seen Garfield on the witness stand, but also how he and Allee had put on a phony act for the grand jury:

Now, when they did this before the grand jury, they put
on quite a show. Because as the record of this trial shows—

apart from the grand-jury minutes that were read in here, where Mr. Patrusky says he was telling the truth—he didn't just identify Mr. Garfield. He was first shown pictures of somebody else. He looks at it and says: "Oh, no, that's not the man who was being cross-examined. This man whose picture you are showing me has thick dark hair. That's not the man I described. I described a little bald man." Show him another picture. "Ah, that's the one. Sam Garfield."

Mr. Brill brought out on cross-examination that he had already said that he was going to say it was Garfield when he was down in the prosecutor's office. All of this before the grand jury—of showing him another picture and having him say, "That's not him," and then in the next picture, "Ah, that's it; that's the one"—that's a little stage play. Like the stage play put on before you from the witness stand at this trial.

I was ultimately able to dismiss the counts charging that I had paid Patrusky:

So, as to the two payments which allegedly took place—thank goodness we have been able to prove by outside incontrovertible, indisputable evidence, that they never could have taken place; that the circumstances surrounding them given by Mr. Patrusky were nothing but a pack of lies.

The jury seemed to enjoy in particular the summary of the saga of Patrusky's tax return: how he reported the money as indicated by his work sheet prepared in 1964 until we decided to test it for aging, at which point it turned out to have been prepared in 1969 from records stolen from Herbie Weinstein's car. As I told the story, I sensed that the jurors felt they were watching a mystery story unfold, and in a sense they were. I couldn't help being relaxed and even sarcastic as I tried to capture the spirit of Patrusky's inventiveness. The jury, I could see, was reliving Patrusky's phoniness and was treating his squirming from one lie to another with amused disdain. I was trying to tell the story just as it had come out at the trial, and the amusing side of it overtook the seriousness of his lies as we followed Patrusky's story into the trunk of Weinstein's car:

"Do you remember you told us about . . . the checks, the checkbooks, the canceled checks, and 'me'? So now I guess we better look at those checks and canceled checks, and maybe we can look and see how legitimate this is, and the other things you produced and said, might be. So will you please produce your checkbooks and your canceled checks?"

Well, he didn't quite make that one!

"What happened to them?"

"Well, you see, back in 1966—check with the police, they will tell you—the car was stolen. My partner, Mr. Weinstein, had these particular records in the car. . . ."

(Mr. Weinstein always carried around in the trunk of his car Mr. Patrusky's 1964 tax work papers.)

". . . They were in the trunk of his car. It was parked in front of the supermarket, and he came out of the supermarket, the car was stolen. He reported it to the police. Not only that, he reported it to the insurance company."

. . . in the middle of Mr. Garlock's cross-examination, Mr. Perito stood up and said, "Proof of loss, here it is."

We examined it later and we offered it in evidence. . . .

And this proof of loss and report details what was taken from the car. And the funny thing is this—it does list a lot of records that they say were taken, but it did *not* list the records Mr. Patrusky says were taken. It has "Semel and Patrusky books of original account, general ledgers, subsidiary ledgers, Patrusky and Weinstein schedules" of something or other, "breakdowns" of something or other (it looks like checks), "Harry Graff, Inc., clients' inventory records," and so on and so forth. And on the bottom at the end, "miscellaneous schedules, documents, records," so on and so forth.

We are not interested in Mr. Graff's inventory records. We

ing all over the lunch table I finally got the job done as best I
could.

We arrived back in court, and after all the cutting and re-
arranging, I was almost disappointed when the judge advised
me that he had decided not to curtail my time! Now I had to
spend the next ten minutes before court convened trying to
restore some of the material I had eliminated.

Despite this confusion, the afternoon was more interesting
than the morning, as I reached the relationship of Weisman,
the "victim" of the criminal extortion, and Roy Cohn, the extorter:

> But you come to something that almost defies belief, and
> that is this: If somebody criminally extorts—a felony, an of-
> fense that you go to jail for, a crime—extorts, forces you,
> threatens you, puts you in fear, I guess when you see him
> coming down the street, you run the other way.
>
> What is the story?
>
> You know his Honor mentioned at the beginning of the
> case, in talking about the conspiracy charges, "Actions speak
> louder than words," and indeed they do. Actions and writings
> speak louder than words.
>
> What was Mr. Weisman's attitude toward me, a man who
> . . . "criminally extorted" him?
>
> Did he run away? Was he denouncing me all over the place?
> What happened?
>
> It starts about two weeks after the alleged "extortion." He
> got married. Gay, his wife, and he went off on their honey-
> moon. And then he received a telegram, Exhibit AK, from
> the criminal extorters, Mr. Kiser and me.

The friendly writings from the one I had supposedly extorted
were stacked in front of me on the table that separated me
from the jury box. I picked them up and held each in my
raised hand for the jury to see as I recounted them. I read
the telegram:

Mr. Lawrence I. Weisman. Heartiest good wishes for a successful merger. Roy, John Kiser and Mort.

I suppose you would think that an indignant letter came back saying, "How dare you, you people, John Kiser, don't even talk to me," or something like that.

A letter did come from Rome. Exhibit L shows that apparently rather than a bitter complaint about the effrontery of criminal extortioners sending him a telegram, there was an invitation to get together with him and his new wife when they returned to the States.

I replied to that—Exhibit 11, March 19, 1964, Exhibit L in evidence:

Mr. and Mrs. Lawrence I. Weisman, et cetera.
Dear Gay and Larry, I do very much appreciate your nice note from Rome and look forward to seeing you both on your return. Sincerely.

I suppose the letter should bear "Sincerely, your friendly blackmailer," or something.

I had finished with the documents establishing Weisman's friendly conduct toward me, but there was something else I was going to hold up in front of the jury as I finished the story of my relationship with the man I had supposedly extorted:

. . . as my learned friend Mr. Garlock would say, there is a *pièce de résistance*—very shortly before Mr. Weisman came down to tell the grand jury that I was a criminal extorter and blackmailer.

As I spoke the words, I could hear some activity in back of me. I knew that it was Tom Bolan unpacking the silver pitcher. He met me halfway as I stepped back from the jury box. He handed me the pitcher, and I raised it to the jury:

One very pleasant happy day, I received a pitcher, which is not in evidence, but the inscription on it is—and twelve cups —from the victim of the criminal extortion and blackmail, to the criminal extorter and blackmailer. The inscription says,

R M C
To the Second Best Lawyer
In the United States
With Regard and Affection
of
LIW—No. 1

Now, of course you always have the highest regard and affection for the man who criminally extorted and blackmailed you. I will say I am sure I am nowhere near number two as a lawyer, but if he wants to put himself a notch ahead of me, he is right. I am here and he is not.

I looked at the big clock on the courtroom wall. The time had come for me to speak those closing words I had so carefully thought out:

There is one final thought that I wish to share with you.

His Honor will undoubtedly instruct you that an indictment is nothing, no evidence of guilt. It is a formal way of bringing a charge, having issue joined in a criminal case, joined by a plea of not guilty, and then tried before you. But as a formalistic matter, the indictment, as Mr. Brill told you in the opening, does read, "The United States of America against Roy Cohn" and others.

I do not believe for one second that the United States of America is against me, John Kiser, or John Curtin. The mere concept bothers me as much as anything in the world.

As I was thinking of that concept and looking over the record preparing to address you, I came across a quote which Judge Wyatt gave to the jury on one of those days. I think it was one of the early days of Mr. Brill's illness. It was a quote from Ecclesiastes, and the quote began, I remember, "It is better the ending of a thing than the beginning thereof."

I tried to apply that to this case and I thought of the beginning of the case and the beginning was the testimony of Lawrence Weisman. He was the first witness called by the Government. Lawrence Weisman lied to the grand jury. Lawrence Weisman said he sold the stock because he was extorted until he came back under cross-examination and admitted all these other reasons for the sale, all these reasons for the sale of the stock. Lawrence Weisman who, after all these exhibits you have had read to you and seen this afternoon, says I criminally extorted and blackmailed him. That was the beginning.

Then I thought of the end. I remember when one of the members of the prosecution's staff stood up and said, "The United States of America rests," and just before that statement was made, a witness had walked off the stand, the ending witness, and that man was Bernard Patrusky. He was the ending witness. Bernard Patrusky, who admitted lying to two grand juries, who did lie to a third one, and who did lie to you here in this courtroom; who produced Exhibit X, and everything else you heard about here.

So, that was the ending. Well, I thought back on the quotation from Ecclesiastes, and despite, I am sure, its cogency and validity, it was a little difficult for me to see how the ending with Patrusky was very much better than the beginning with Weisman. But then I realized two things. I realized that Weisman and Patrusky are not the United States of America: In this case, as the sole judges of the facts, as the only people in the world representing our system of law and justice, who pass on the facts and the truth under a system of law the finest known to mankind, devised in a country which a lot of people like to knock, but I know which we all believe is the greatest country in the world, under that system you are the sole representatives of the United States of America in passing upon the facts and the truth in this case.

And then I realized the second thing: I realized that the end had not come when Bernard Patrusky walked off that witness stand. I realized that the end can come only when you have spoken and rendered your verdict, and I hope and know, if you will, I pray, that when that end does come it will indeed be better and brighter than was the beginning.

I had determined not to show any sign of emotion, but I knew that as I approached the end of the summation, it would be hard not to. I was doing fine until the last few words. I looked up and my eyes met those of a lady juror in the front row. I saw tears in hers. There were soon a few in mine.

The next day Allee read his entire summation from a notebook on a lectern. It's no fun sitting there for a whole day listening to someone declaiming what a dangerous public enemy you are. Despite this, I was not disturbed by Allee's summation. The jury seemed rather grim and unimpressed. They did not seem to react sympathetically to some of Allee's arguments, such as his attempt to belittle Weisman's friendliness toward me after my "extortion":

> Take the United States of America, for example. In the 1950's the United States of America became good friends with Germany and became good friends with Japan.
>
> Does that prove that the Second World War was never fought? Of course not. Times change. Situations change. Pressures change. People sometimes are enemies and become friends again. And that is all that evidence proves. It doesn't prove there was no extortion.

He forgot that the United States hadn't become bosom buddies of Hitler and Tojo and that Weisman and I aren't members of the United Nations.

Perhaps Allee's least effective argument was that what we had brought out about the prosecution witnesses was like merely showing a grease spot on a tie, and that we were asking the jury to consider the grease spot (which was really nothing to bother a sensible person) rather than the tie. He argued to the jury:

Another smoke screen relates to a technique that I would call the grease-on-the-necktie technique. You look at your necktie and you look closer and closer and closer until you have the necktie right up to your eye, until all you can see is the grease spot, and you say that is not a tie, that is a grease spot.

I noticed Tom break into a grin during this agrument. He said afterward: "That is about the silliest point I ever heard. I can't think of anything more annoying or distasteful than a grease spot glaring out from one's necktie. I wonder who spilled that one on Allee."

That night, with nothing to do, I felt unemployed. Still under great tension I wanted nothing more than to escape from all thought of the trial. I remembered that three years before during a blizzard in Chicago a girl I know brought two actors to a party I gave for my mother. They were Donal Donnelly and Patrick Bedford. At that time they starred in *Philadelphia, Here I Come!* They had been wonderful to my mother. Autographed pictures followed our visit, and they wrote to her in Gaelic, which she asked the Irish ambassador to translate. This night, three years later—December 11, 1969—the night before my case was to go to the jury, Don was directing and Patrick was starring in a new show by Brian Friel, *The Mundy Scheme.* It was opening night, and strange as it might seem, I wanted to see the show. It would have been hypocritical of me not to go; I was not yet ready to go into mourning. I called the box office and got a balcony seat for the show, which I enjoyed immensely.

At intermission I ran into Mitzi and Sam Newhouse. Sam greeted me: "You must be crazy. What are you doing here?" Mitzi, my defense counsel, said, "Sam, leave him alone. He's probably studying their techniques to use in court."

The next morning began the final day of the trial. Instead of a two-hour charge on the law as expected, the judge reviewed the facts—90 percent of them drawn from the direct testimony of prosecution witnesses—and didn't finish until after 5 P.M. Tom and I thought he tried to kill me. But Tom said, "Look at the jury." I did, and they looked like their capacity for absorption had been taxed beyond human endurance after four days of oratory. I didn't blame them, and I worried less.

The jury received the case shortly before dinner. Their first note came before they went to eat. It requested some exhibits on the first count, dealing with Curtin, and their request told us two things: (1) They were going down the indictment count by count. (2) The requested evidence was favorable to us, as it had been highlighted by Curtin's lawyer, Dick Owen, in his summation.

We went to dinner at a small Italian restaurant. Most of the people from my office were there. So were such old friends as Fay and Willie Levine, and Ann Frank, whose husband had given me the idea of getting a job in the United States Attorney's office in 1948. I was under too much tension to eat, and I tried to cover up my feeling by joking with three newspapermen at the next table: Scott Schmedel, of the *Wall Street Journal;* Bob Evans, of UPI; and Arnold Lubasch, of *The New York Times.* Through the years Scott and Bob, along with Norma Abrams, of the *Daily News,* had covered many of the cases I had tried and those in which I had been tried.

After dinner we walked back to the courthouse. It was a Friday night. The usual jury deathwatch was on. The press were grumbling about the interrupted weekend. Allee's wife had joined him in the courtroom. Morgenthau's executive assistant headed the list of members of his staff waiting the night out.

Si Newhouse and some other friends began to make the usual predictions about the jury's decision. This time I agreed with Tom. We both believed that the jury would not be out overnight and that we would win. Significantly, none of the jurors had brought overnight bags or asked about them, and many lived in outlying counties. Nor did they request a single exhibit suggested by the prosecution.

The second note from the jury asked for the diaries of Tom Bolan and Bill Cassidy. We had strongly stressed them to support our position that my disclosure meeting with Larkin about Reicher's misconduct took place before the alleged extortion of Weisman. No request could have been more favorable. This note came about 9:35 P.M. An hour later, while I was pacing the corridor, I noticed that people close to the courtroom door began moving quickly inside. The courteous and friendly courtroom bailiff, Joe Beneducci, gripped my arm. "It's a verdict," he said. We all went inside.

When the jury was brought into the courtroom and sat in the box awaiting the judge's arrival, something peculiar happened. The courtroom legend is that when a verdict is favorable, the jurors look reassuringly at the defendant. Not one of them looked at me. Even Tom was perplexed. The judge bustled up to the bench. He leaned down and commanded, "Mr. Clerk"—which was the instruction for Mr. Beneducci to take the verdict formally.

After the foreman pronounced all defendants not guilty on all counts, all hell broke loose. Well-wishers jumped the barriers. Shouts echoed through the courtroom. The judge's gaveling to order went almost unnoticed.

As I prepared to walk down to the press room to face the cameras and the questions, a young lawyer who had been a frequent spectator at the trial came up to me and whispered, "The winner and still champ."

I felt dazed. About the only coherent thing I said in the press room was "God bless America." I meant it. And I always will.

VII

The Prosecution:
Methods and Motives

THE PROSECUTOR'S MOTIVES should be the same in every case: the impartial enforcement of the law, the protection of the innocent, the exposure of the guilty. But it doesn't always work that way. Too many prosecutors have other motives. There are those like Jim Garrison in New Orleans who are obsessed with a theory—untenable as it might be —and willing to go to any length to prove it. Then there are prosecutors who are just out for headlines; some people think all of them are, but this is not so. There have been prosecutors' offices that are run with quiet efficiency. When J. Edward Lumbard, now chief judge of the United States Court of Appeals for the Second Circuit, was United States Attorney for the Southern District of New York, publicity was never a consideration. Then there are some prosecutors with political motives, who use their power to assist their political supporters and to make trouble for their detractors. And there are prosecutors who have personal motives and use their public power to even up old scores.

This commentary might be of interest from an academic view, but it can also be of deadly significance for a defendant who ends up indicted, on trial—and perhaps in jail—as a result of prosecutorial muscle. Any defendant faces the problem of overcoming a possible feeling on the part of the jury that where there's smoke, there must be fire. If the grand jury indicted the defendant, and if the "Government" is prosecuting him, he must be bad in some way. If it can be established that the prosecution is motivated by personal malice, this is highly relevant. For example, if a deal has been made with certain defendants to testify against others, it is appropriate to point out, if apt, that without personal motives it would make no sense for the prosecutor to have made such a deal. This rationale might not be applicable if, for example, a "deal" is made to extend leniency to a minor participant in a serious crime in order to insure the conviction of a murderer or dope peddler. The jury should be permitted to weigh the seriousness of the crimes of those who got off free against those the defendant is charged with. If the result makes no sense from this standpoint, then improper motive becomes a possibility. But most courts recoil at the thought of "trying the prosecution." Note, for instance, Judge Wyatt's reaction to Ed Garlock's opening remarks:

GARLOCK: . . . Theoretically the Government is under a duty to present all the facts to you. The Government is supposed to have an interest in justice and justice requires the presentation of all the facts. It may very well be, as my brother [counsel] Brill said yesterday, that the United States of America is not against these defendants, but I think the course of this trial will show that the prosecutor is against these defendants.

ALLEE: Objection.

GARLOCK: Because—

THE COURT: Yes, Mr. Garlock, I will not permit such remarks to this jury. We are not here to try the prosecutors.

GARLOCK: No. No, your Honor doesn't understand what I'm getting at. I am getting—

THE COURT: I understand enough to tell you that that matter will not be gone into.

GARLOCK: I was referring only to the deliberate selection of favorable evidence by the prosecutor.

THE COURT: I will not permit that. I have no evidence of it. There has been no evidence yet.

GARLOCK: I say I will demonstrate it, your Honor.

THE COURT: I direct you to drop that subject.

My experience is that the prosecutor's motivation does manage to get across to the jury in most instances. Sometimes this is accomplished by the judge who is trying to exclude it. At my 1969 trial Judge Wyatt said so loudly and so often that Morgenthau's alleged vendetta against me was no issue that I'm sure everyone concluded it was a very important one.

While the Court would not permit us to ask about Morgenthau's animus toward me directly, indirectly it became apparent. One may always ask a witness on cross-examination about his motives for testifying against the defendant. And one of the strongest motives is to save his own neck. So a cross-examiner had an indisputable right to ask a witness about any deal he has made with the prosecution for clemency in return for testifying. Such deals center around getting no jail sentence or a much lighter one than the offense might justify. If a witness has been indicted in a multicount indictment, which is usual, the deal with the prosecution might include acceptance of a plea to only one of the counts and dismissal of the others, thus limiting the possible sentence.

It is in asking questions of the witness who made the deal that the prosecution's motive appears. If "deals" are made with six or seven people charged with major crimes so that they will testify against Cohn, whose alleged participation is minor, one may strongly suspect that the prosecutor offering the deals is out to get Cohn. Usually a common-sense inference must be drawn, as a direct admission is rare. Prosecution witnesses almost ritualistically lie on the question of whether they have made a deal, because often part of the deal is that it will be denied so as not to detract from the credibility of the witnesses. (The prosecutor usually closes the deal with the witness by saying, "Of course, no promises are being made to you.") They stoutly maintain that they have no commitment; that by cooperating they will escape jail in pending criminal cases in which they are involved. They emphatically deny any promise to them by the prosecution. Almost always, they are lying through their teeth— with the prosecutor sitting there knowing that they are. And I'm sure the judge suspects they are.

A reasonably intelligent witness is customarily coached by his own lawyer on how to handle the ticklish matter of cross-examination. Imagine the lawyer for the witness explaining to him the night before he testifies: "Now, listen carefully. In cross-examination they will ask you if you have a deal for lenient treatment for yourself because you're testifying for the prosecution. Your answer, of course, is No."

"Well, what if they ask why I'm testifying?"

"Tell them because you have decided to tell the truth— that you want a clear conscience."

"What if they ask about my meetings with the prosecutors?"

"Say that all they did was ask you what the facts are, and tell you to tell the truth. Another question they'll ask you is if you expect a suspended sentence in your own case. You answer that they told you sentencing is all up to the judge, and no one can tell what's going to happen."

Some lawyers, or witnesses on their own volition without prompting from their lawyers, carry the act too far. Congenital liars and con men often forget their lines someplace along the way and mess up in the role of a "reformed" man testifying for pure truth's sake. Sam Garfield was not very convincing in this role:

> RAICHLE: And without that hope and without that expectation [of leniency] you wouldn't have told the story that you told here, would you?
>
> GARFIELD: That's not so.
>
> RAICHLE: What?
>
> GARFIELD: That's not so.
>
> RAICHLE: How many people did you swindle in the Shawano case?
>
> GARFIELD: Oh, I don't know.
>
> . . .
>
> RAICHLE: You are not testifying here through the remorse of conscience, then?
>
> . . .
>
> GARFIELD: I don't understand what you mean.
>
> RAICHLE: You don't know what a "remorse of conscience" means?
>
> GARFIELD: Yes, sir.
>
> RAICHLE: Do you know what "conscience" means?
>
> GARFIELD: Yes, sir.
>
> RAICHLE: Does your conscience bother you because you swindled all these people? Yes or no.
>
> GARFIELD: No.

When asked whether he expected to escape jail, he said he had "no idea" that he would not receive a sentence.

A friend of mine read an account of this testimony and asked: "Would a man who expected to go to jail buy thirty suits at two hundred and fifty dollars per suit and six dozen shirts?" To which I replied: "Are you kidding? Of course not. Who did that?" My friend said: "I was up at my tailor's, and he mentioned that he was rushing an order of thirty suits and six dozen shirts for Sam Garfield." I knew what an impact something like that would have on the jury.

What better way to show that someone knew he wasn't about to be sent off to a long jail term than by proving he just bought himself a large new wardrobe? We immediately checked the information and subpoenaed the tailor. We never had to use him. Frank Raichle handled the matter on Garfield's cross-examination.

He first had Garfield repeat that he had no idea that he would escape jail for his confessed crimes, in return for testifying against me. Raichle then confronted Garfield with his recent order of thirty suits and six dozen shirts. An astonished Garfield tried to indicate that the number of suits and shirts was slightly on the high side. The jury could hardly have been impressed by his point that he only ordered twenty-four suits instead of thirty, or four dozen shirts instead of six dozen. Raichle's final thrust was: "Don't you think the styles might have changed by the time you got out of jail?" This incident was a dramatic way of demonstrating that although the witness's words denied a deal to keep himself out of jail, his own actions belied his words.

To bolster Garfield's and Swann's denial of the hotel-suite meeting with Murray Gottesman and me, the prosecution produced Hyman Lehrich and Sidney Barkley. All they had to say was that they hung around Garfield's suite at the Pierre from time to time but had never seen Gottesman and me there together and in fact had never met Gottesman. Since no one had ever said that either Lehrich or Barkley was present or had ever met Gottesman, their testimony was somewhat less than persuasive. Indeed, Lehrich, supposedly an experienced lawyer, committed one of the cardinal errors on the witness stand: He was a wise guy and tried to fence with defense counsel.

At the first 1964 trial we didn't even cross-examine them, but this turned out to have been a mistake; jurors are apparently disturbed by the failure to cross-examine a witness. In the retrial we did not repeat the mistake. We cross-examined

Lehrich and Barkley. It became clear that as a reward for their negative testimony, they were both to escape jail for conspiracy to swindle in the United Dye case. Lehrich, a lawyer, was not even indicted. He was named a conspirator in the fraud. Barkley was indicted in both the United Dye swindle and another stock-fraud case and pleaded guilty, but he was not sentenced until after he had delivered for Morgenthau by testifying against me. And for his insignificant testimony that he didn't see us at a meeting when no one said he did, he escaped jail for his part in the United Dye swindle.

Actually, he had something else going for him at the same time. In 1958 Barkley's lawyer, Leonard Glass, told him he had an opportunity to become an assistant United States Attorney in the securities section. Barkley told him to take the job, and he did. By 1959 he was actually the assistant in charge of the United Dye investigation, the prosecutor actually presenting the evidence to the grand jury, weighing the indictment of Garfield. In August, 1959, Barkley had secret meetings with him and even brought him to Garfield's hotel suite. Glass, the federal prosecutor, had breakfast with Garfield, the prospective defendant.

A couple of days later Glass slipped to Barkley a manila pad containing in Glass's own handwriting the actual questions that another prospective defendant, Swann, was to be asked before the grand jury. Barkley testified before the grand jury on June 8, 1962, that Glass had said: "Give these to Swann before he comes in to testify and let him study them and answer them properly. These will be the questions that I'm going to ask him, and also tell him, you know, you can tell him that he'll be treated properly when he gets into the grand-jury room; that he doesn't have anything to worry about."

Barkley gave these questions to Swann in Garfield's suite in the presence of Lehrich. After Swann testified before the secret grand-jury session, Glass promptly reported the grand jury's reaction to convicted swindler Barkley, who in turn clued in Garfield and Swann. Later, Barkley accompanied Glass on a trip to Beverly Hills and Las Vegas. Garfield paid them for the trip in cash. Barkley bought clothes for Glass in Las Vegas. Garfield "loaned" Barkley over $37,000 in cash, which was never paid back. The *Wall Street Journal* reported the situation:

> Jurors at the trial of Roy M. Cohn were told Leonard Glass, a Government prosecutor in 1959, provided an advance list of questions so a prospective defendant in the United Dye & Chemical Corp. stock fraud case could plan his testimony before a 1959 Federal grand jury. . . .
>
> In 1959, Mr. Glass was an assistant U.S. Attorney for the Southern District of New York, and was in charge of presenting evidence to a grand jury investigating possible fraud in connection with United Dye.
>
> Barkley said that on Aug. 18, 1959, he obtained from Mr. Glass a list of questions the prosecutor intended to ask Swann before the grand jury on Aug. 20. On Aug. 19, Barkley continued, Swann, Garfield, Hyman D. Lehrich, a United Dye attorney, and he went over the questions. . . .
>
> Garfield also said he loaned Barkley large sums of money in 1959 and 1960 and financed a trip Barkley and Mr. Glass allegedly made to California and Las Vegas in September 1959. . . .

Yet who wound up on trial—Garfield and Barkley? Certainly not. I did. Of course, at first, they all denied deals. But to our advantage was their own stupidity: They apparently never thought to keep their mouths shut. For instance, an investigator located a former secretary of Swann's in Evansville, Indiana, named Margaret Garvey. She related how Swann bragged about how he would walk off with a fine, which is just what happened: "Mr. Swann came into the office and I bid him the time of day and I commented that I had not seen him around Evansville for some time, and he said, 'No, I have been out of town. I have been in New York in the trial of a case. I violated some of the Security Acts. I pleaded guilty. I will not get a jail sentence but I will get a fine.' "

I can imagine the jury's reaction to this, after hearing Swann's testimony: "I have not asked the district attorney anything about what he is going to do because I was informed by him in the beginning that he made no promises of any kind to me or any character in connection with any testimony that I might give, and I knew it would be a foolish question to go back and ask him after I had already been told that."

Some of the proof I have that the 1964 trial was simply an outgrowth of Morgenthau's personal antagonism comes from the testimony of Larry Weisman at my 1969 trial. Weisman was about the only witness who didn't lie about having made a deal. He couldn't. Luck was on our side when he held out for formal immunity, which was a matter of official record. And since, under law, immunity does not cover future perjury (or future crimes in general), Weisman invariably became very cautious when questioned about events of which other persons had knowledge, such as Morgenthau's offer of deals to people in trouble themselves in return for saying something against me. Other witnesses at the 1969 trial were not as candid as Weisman in admitting the deal. Edward Krock, guilty of swindling hundreds of thousands of dollars, after describing thirty long sessions with Morgenthau's staff, shouted: "I could not get a cup of coffee from them!" But I'm sure he knew that by giving me the business he could get a suspended sentence from them. He pleaded guilty in another courtroom the very day he testified against me. At his allocution (the proceedings on pleading) his lawyer was asked the usual question by the judge as to whether Krock understood what he was doing. The lawyer replied: "Oh, yes. I've told Mr. Krock it was in his best personal interests to change his plea at this time." A few hours later at my trial Krock denied he had a deal. We obtained the minutes of the allocution some days later and read them to the jury.

Krock's cohort, Victor Muscat, also tried to lie about his deal. His problem, like Swann's, was a big mouth. One Sunday in early winter of 1968 Patty Burns and her husband, Ned, went to the Giants' pro-football game at Yankee Stadium. They were seated next to their friends, Happy and Victor Muscat. Muscat had recently been indicted for perjury and false filings with the Securities and Exchange Commission, and when the subject came up, he explained to the Burnses: "I have nothing to worry about. I'm not going to jail. All they want from me is to help them hang Roy Cohn. Everything is all set."

After the Burnses returned to their Greenwich home, Patty had her daily chat with one of her close friends: "How was the game?" "Oh, very exciting." "Who was there?" "Well, we sat with Happy and Victor Muscat." "Isn't he in a lot of trouble?" "Oh, no, he's all set. He's made a deal to help them get Roy Cohn and he's not going to get a jail sentence."

That night Patty's friend had her customary telephone chat with Vonnie O'Brian, the pretty wife of columnist-commentator Jack O'Brian: "What's new?" "Oh, I was talking to Patty. Did you know that Vic Muscat made a deal not to go to jail in return for testifying against Roy?" Von replied, "No —and I wonder if Roy knows it." A few minutes later I did.

In November, 1969, after Victor Muscat took the witness stand against me and swore, under cross-examination, that he had been given no indication that he would escape jail by testifying against me, we asked if he had ever told anyone that he had made such a deal. Of course not. The judge, in his anteroom out of Muscat's hearing, asked where this line of questioning was leading. Brill told him and advised that we were subpoenaing the Muscats' friend, Patty Burns, to whom he had bragged about his deal. Having responded to the judge's inquiry in front of Allee and Perito, Brill then asked the Court to direct them not to hint to Muscat that we were calling Mrs. Burns. Obviously we did not want her pressured by him. The Court gave Perito and Allee such a direction. This was Friday afternoon.

On Sunday night I received a call from Vonnie O'Brian. Vonnie had received a call from Patty's friend, who had received a hysterical call from Patty Burns. Patty had received a call from Muscat. He knew everything. She was going to be called to testify. Monday morning, court opened. Muscat was back on the stand for resumption of cross-examination. Brill asked if he had talked with Allee and Perito after court on Friday. Yes, he had. What had they said? They had told him that Patty Burns was going to be subpoenaed by us to tell of his admission of a deal. What did he do? He called Patty Burns.

This brazen flouting of the Court's direction to Perito and Allee not to tip off Muscat went unpunished, although the Court acknowledged what had happened: "It does not affect the course of the trial, and I don't think we'd better interrupt the course of the trial to consider this any further here." If tables had been reversed and we had disobeyed, I am not sure that we would have gotten off as lightly. Any further chance of developing the matter was crushed when the judge decided to rule that in any event he would exclude Mrs. Burns's testimony as not proper rebuttal—whatever that might mean.

The prosecutor has the power to play God. Under no control he can sit there and decide who should get the axe and who should be spared. William F. Buckley, Jr., described Morgenthau's conduct after my latest indictment:

> . . . here is merely one more offensive by a punchdrunk official who remembers that he is supposed to keep on charging for as

long as he can stand up and who somewhere along the way in the mists of time came to identify the defense of the law with the persecution of Roy Cohn.

An unscrupulous prosecutor can and does use his power to make deals with criminals in order to get a personal enemy. Murray Kempton, in a column that far from flatters me, put it this way:

> Thanks to the rules for corroboration, a common pattern is for one thief to be convicted and two fellow thieves to go free for testifying against him. This places upon the prosecutor a great responsibility for selection; he must look at three criminals and decide which deserves the worst punishment. . . . The system is just too open to selections rendered on simple personal distaste. . . .

When Stanley Fuld, now the chief judge of New York, was a prosecutor, he was noted for his sense of justice and his concern for truth. He would often confound prosecutorial circles by standing up in court and confessing an error if he felt a defendant's rights had been violated. How to instill this code of honor into prosecutors who want to win even at the expense of suborning perjury and concealing the truth might be more of an ethical problem than a legal one. But there is no reason that some minimum standards of professional honor cannot be devised.

"Do you regret any of your actions as counsel for the McCarthy Committee?" That is the question most often asked of me in interviews or after a speech at a college or law school. I answer that after fifteen years it would be folly to say I would do everything the same way, but by and large the McCarthy "methods" were not so fierce as generally portrayed, and, moreover, they gain in stature by comparison with the way other committees and grand juries operate today.

But no one ever asks: "Do you regret any of your actions as a young prosecutor on the staff of the United States Attorney?" This question would be more troublesome. I do not regret my role in the prosecution of the Rosenberg atom spy trial. The Rosenbergs were guilty of one of the most serious of crimes—treason. In trying the case the prosecution presented factual evidence—evidence obtained fairly, without intercepting anyone's mail or tapping anyone's phone. Evidence obtained from accomplice witnesses—who in all cases were less involved than the Rosenbergs—was corroborated by disinterested witnesses.

But I cannot reply with the same degree of equanimity about some of the mass conspiracy trials I prosecuted. I think of cases where five, ten, fifteen, or twenty defendants were all lumped together in a narcotics "conspiracy" trial, and how they would be sent off to prison for five, ten, fifteen, or twenty years on the word of some accomplice witness sitting on the stand and pointing at one defendant after another, uttering the one sentence about "participation" that under federal law is enough to open the prison gates. Experience has left me rather cynical about the validity of accomplice-witness testimony and about conspiracy trials in general.

Many young and inexperienced prosecutors are hard-nosed. They are ambitious and often feel that winning is more important than serving justice. They have not yet learned to see the "other side," to see that winning is not everything, to see which values really count.

I was prosecuted by young and inexperienced men; for them, getting me was more important than truth, fair play, and even obeying the law. They worked for a demanding boss, who expected them to come back with the opponent's head. One of my young tormentors from Morgenthau's staff had a member of his immediate family prosecuted by Morgenthau after my first acquittal. He is reported to have commented: "He never forgave me for not getting Cohn."

One might think that had Morgenthau been so interested in seeing me behind bars, he would have prosecuted me personally. But in his eight years as United States Attorney, he never tried a case. This defied the almost unbroken tradition of working United States Attorneys who didn't send in others to do their errands. One thinks of Judge Lumbard; John F. X. McGohey, later a federal judge; Irving H. Saypol and Myles J. Lane, now state supreme court justices; and George L. Medalie, Martin Conboy, John T. Cahill, and Paul Williams—all working United States Attorneys. But Morgenthau's policy was to "sic 'em" with young and inexperienced assistants while he burrowed in his fourth-floor suite.

The prosecution is the "protector of the innocent," as the radio program used to tell us. And the United States Supreme Court agrees. In *Berger v. United States* the Court held that a United States Attorney's duty is not only to prosecute the guilty but to protect the rights of the accused. Gerald Walpin, Morgenthau's assistant prosecutor at my first trial, and Allee and Perito at my second did not appear to heed this admonition.

Walpin played a role in the interception of my mail and Tom Bolan's mail, a matter that caused a stir when it was publicly revealed. The story of how we found out about this interception is interesting: Tom Bolan has lived with his family in Cambria Heights, a suburb of New York City in Queens County, since postwar days. Their mail is normally delivered every morning by Charlie, but one day Charlie was sick, and a substitute carrier rang the bell. When Mrs. Bolan came out to get the mail, she found the substitute carrier scratching his head and studying a yellow card. He handed it to Mrs. Bolan, saying that he didn't understand what it meant. Mrs. Bolan did. It was a confidential direction to the mail carrier to deliver the Bolans' mail to his supervisor.

Early in the United Dye case we were told by a highly

reliable but unusable source that my mail was being secretly intercepted by Morgenthau. But how could we ever prove it? Were it not for that substitute carrier, we probably never could have.

On the basis of the document handed Mrs. Bolan we immediately moved to quash the indictment on the ground that the mail of my lawyer, Tom Bolan, was being intercepted. Walpin flatly denied any knowledge of or responsibility for this in a sworn affidavit, and Morgenthau put in an affidivit supporting him, but Federal Judge Dawson, to whom my case had been assigned for all purposes, ordered a hearing. Under direct questioning by Judge Dawson, Walpin admitted he not only knew of the mail cover but also had ordered it himself. And not only was Tom's home mail being intercepted, but so was mine, both at the office and at my home.

Judge Dawson exploded in comments that made the front pages, calling the prosecutor's conduct in intercepting the mail of a defendant and his lawyer after an indictment "shocking," "terrible," and "stupid" and saying it "smacks of Russia rather than the United States." Judge Dawson, however, would not dismiss the indictment: Like many judges, he felt that controversial cases should be resolved by a jury, not on the basis of a technicality.

Morgenthau was severely criticized in the press and by certain legislators, and even my old foe, the American Civil Liberties Union, came to my defense and condemned Morgenthau (in fact, someone from the A.C.L.U. later told me they were glad I was acquitted so they could go back to hating me). They issued the following statement:

> According to news reports that have not been denied, an Assistant U.S. Attorney intimated in a statement to the Court that his office had not ordered a check on mail addressed to Roy Cohn or his attorney, Mr. Bolan. In doing so, he misled the Court and was guilty of an inexcusable evasion and lack

of candor. The failure of the U.S. Attorney to reprimand his assistant's flagrant violation of the lawyer's ethical duty or to replace him in the prosecution of the case may be construed as condonation.

We believe an inquiry should be conducted by the Grievance Committee of the Bar Association.

Another Morgenthau assistant, Albert J. Gaynor, combined Morgenthau's vindictiveness with Walpin's brazenness. He had his own special brand of arrogance and was roundly defeated when he ran for public office in Westchester County. His law firm, which continued to carry his name while he was a federal prosecutor, also continued to represent people under investigation in Morgenthau's office, and this evoked a rather caustic editorial in the Yonkers *Herald Statesman* entitled "Let's Have Some Answers to Puzzling Questions": "There is the question of the propriety of the continued use of Mr. Gaynor's name in the title of a law firm representing a company whose activities, in some broad aspects, are said to be under scrutiny by the federal prosecutor to whom Mr. Gaynor is a principal aide."

Walpin's tactics were repeated by Perito in my 1969 trial. Indeed, the two men were similar in several respects. Both were but a little over five feet tall, both had gone to Harvard, both had irritating personalities, and both had the annoying habit of making constant Halloween-mask faces during testimony or objections to convey their anger or annoyance at what was being said. They can drive the most tolerant judge up the wall, and I'm sure that their negative personalities created less than a favorable impression on jurors. Judge Dawson had a fiery temper, so his calling Walpin "stupid" isn't of more than passing significance. But even one with so equable a temper as Judge Bonsal, who presided at the second 1964 trial, could finally contain himself no longer and ordered Walpin to sit down and to stop his constant head-bobbing.

And in the 1969 trial Judge Wyatt, who hardly looked with disfavor on anyone on the prosecution staff, almost gave up on Perito—albeit for messing up the prosecution's case. (I hasten to add that not all of Morgenthau's assistants were of this ilk. The fairness of some, such as Andrew J. Maloney and John Doyle, is well recognized.)

Perito had conducted the grand-jury investigation of me for a year and a half. As an example of his fairness, when he called Patrusky as a witness against me, he failed to bring to the attention of the grand jury that indicted me in 1969 the fact that Patrusky had told two completely opposite stories to the previous two grand juries he faced. How could a grand jury evaluate Patrusky's credibility as a witness when the prosecution concealed from it the fact that he obviously lied in at least one of his previous grand-jury appearances on the same subject? Of course, we did not find out about this until months later at the trial, as grand-jury proceedings are secret from all, including the accused. (The only exceptions were the reporters and columnists to whom Morgenthau leaked information.)

Nor could Perito have made any effort to check Patrusky's two outrageous lies about giving me money. On the lie about my having given him three thousand dollars outside of the courtroom, he said that he remembered everything very well: He arrived at court and sat in the last row. The witness on the stand was a short bald man in a dark suit. He would then identify a picture of Sam Garfield as that man. Garfield was under cross-examination by a distinguished-looking lawyer with silver hair. He would then identify a picture of my attorney, Frank Raichle, as that man. A short young man was bobbing up and down making objections. That was obviously Walpin. But the story was a lie, and the picture identifications were phonies.

Under cross-examination at the trial Patrusky admitted that *before* he went into the grand jury, he had already

identified the Garfield picture to Allee. The grand-jury minutes show, however, that Allee helped Patrusky "embellish"
his grand-jury testimony by putting on an act with him. He
showed Patrusky a series of pictures, and Patrusky "spon-
taneously" picked out Garfield and Raichle:

ALLEE: I show you this picture. Is this the man who was on
the witness stand when you were in the courtroom?

PATRUSKY: Oh, no, this man has thick dark hair and is much
younger. He's not the man.

ALLEE: Let the record show this was a picture of William D.
Fugazy.

ALLEE: How about this one then?

PATRUSKY: That's the one. That's the man.

ALLEE: Let the record show the witness has identified a picture of Sam Garfield.

Patrusky's second lie about giving me money at my office
was also made with the prosecution's indulgence. Ed Garlock
put it well in his summation:

Now imagine taking the word of a man like Patrusky, a
palpable psychopath, a confessed perjurer, and not taking the
trouble to check and see when Mr. Cohn purchased the Tyson-
Sullivan . . . October . . . 1964. Almost eight months after
the time when Patrusky said Cohn told him he owned it.

Not only that, they didn't even have to find out the date
when Mr. Cohn or Mr. Cohn and his associates acquired or
purchased the Tyson-Sullivan Agency from the estate of Mr.
Sullivan in October; all they had to do was to subpoena the
records of the Tyson-Sullivan Agency to see if they had an
employee, Jerry Howard, at that time. The employment record
was produced here and it showed that Mr. Howard . . . became an employee of that agency after October, 1964.

Now here again we have a total failure of the prosecution to
make the most elementary investigation to test the evidence
upon which they were relying to establish guilt in this case.

Surely, too, the prosecution at the very least must have suspected that the Patrusky "1964" work sheet was manufactured. If they had believed it was authentic, it is inconceivable that they would not have offered it in evidence themselves. A contemporaneous written record made by Patrusky back in 1964 when no motive to invent existed, and which showed receipt of cash, would have been the most damaging evidence against me in the whole case—if true. But the prosecution failed to use it. It was like not having used the stolen State Department reports typed by Hiss and found in the pumpkin on Chambers's farm as evidence against Hiss.

After discovery of the forgery, when Patrusky was claiming that his original records had been "stolen" from the trunk of Weinstein's car and that the insurance proof of loss would support this, Perito dramatically stood up and waved (without actually showing) a piece of paper in front of the jury, saying, "Yes, here it is. I have it right here." (Imagine the reaction if Joe McCarthy had done this with a paper allegedly listing State Department loyalty risks.) By this point in the proceedings Perito's credibility impressed us about as much as Baron von Münchhausen's. But when we demanded to see the document he was waving around, it took us literally days and a court direction to pry it loose from him. And, of course, it contained not one reference to the theft of Patrusky's 1964 work papers. Perito never offered it in evidence as a prosecution exhibit. He just waved it around. Apparently he was hoping to keep it moving too fast for anyone to see it. But Ed Garlock introduced it, and it became John Kiser's Exhibit X. (The phony 1964 work papers also bore the legend Exhibit X, having been introduced by John Curtin's attorney, Dick Owen.)

Garlock summarized the attitude of all of us involved in the defense when he said of our prosecutors: "I should like now to pay my respects to the estimable young men of the prosecution." (At this point I poked Tom Bolan and said, "How can he say that about those scoundrels?"—but Ed soon clarified the issue.)

It will become my duty to say some unkind things about the way this case has been presented and the tactics of the prosecution, but I assure you and I assure them that I bear them no ill will, and I wish them every success—in private practice. . . .

Now, indeed, I couldn't help entertaining certain feelings of sympathy for them as I sat here and watched them struggling and crawling through the sinking sands of their case toward the ever-receding mirage of conviction here. I couldn't help feeling a certain sympathy for them as I saw their carefully pasted, patched structure erode, crumble, and finally collapse.

. . . they were so involved in their preoccupation with proving guilt, so determined to prove it, so contemptuous of anything that was inconsistent with their hypothesis and their assumption, so unwilling to find anything that would contradict that hypothesis, so anxious to accept anything from whatever foul mouth it came that would help their cause. . . .

Justice, it is said, is blind. She is traditionally portrayed as seated on her exalted throne with her eyes bound and holding the scales.

Her eyes are bound so that she cannot be influenced. She is no respecter of persons. Theoretically, at least, she is dealing with a fine, impartial hand equally, for the privileged and the oppressed, the rich and the poor, the high and the low.

But the servants of justice can't blind themselves. The servants of justice have to serve justice and not seek an end that is incompatible with justice.

Justice here required them to make available to you the evidence which contradicted and destroyed their case. Justice required them to be honest with this jury. . . .

What we have here, in my view, is not an example of the administration of justice by the prosecution. The spectacle that has been enacted before you is a spectacle of the arrogant abuse of power. . . .

VIII

The High
Cost of Injustice

Money seems to be our customary barometer for measuring the cost of anything, including injustice. I estimate the dollar cost to me for the six-year official vendetta conducted by Mr. Morgenthau in the name of the United States Government at about $400,000 in actual expense. If added to that is loss of profit from my profession by not having the time to represent available clients and to build up my practice and by losing potential clients who were scared away by the publicity, a total of well over a million dollars would be a conservative estimate of loss. Then I add approximately one penny as my allocable share as an American taxpayer, since I estimate the cost to the taxpayers as a whole for having involuntarily bankrolled Morgenthau's vendetta at over two million dollars. (I would think this an issue that would interest both liberals and conservatives. The former should complain that the money could have been better spent on public welfare projects; the latter, that it would have been better left with the people who earned it.)

For the mistrial, the first trial, and the second my legal fees and purchase of the daily minutes of the courtroom proceedings ran to over $300,000. And the legal fees for cases Morgenthau brought against associates of mine who refused to "cooperate" with him ran to over $36,000. Also, it has cost about $17,000 to duplicate records which have been demanded by Morgenthau's office. My own expenditures were small when compared to the taxpayers' money spent by Morgenthau and company. In no way could we compete with him in money or manpower; he had unlimited access to the public trough for both.

Morgenthau had assigned to him ten special agents of Internal Revenue Service working exclusively on me. It was quite an operation. The squad, known as the Cohn Squad, not content with the results of the mail cover placed on me by Morgenthau's office, put on another one of its own. They intercepted not only my home mail but both incoming and outgoing mail at our law firm, as well as home mail of at least two of my partners. The squad was headed by Agent "Red" Corcoran, who proudly detailed its activities when called to testify before Judge Dawson to explain the mail interception. The culmination of five years' work by this special squad, working in closest liaison as an adjunct to Morgenthau's operation against me, came one morning in 1967, when letter carriers bearing ominous-looking "return receipt requested" epistles from the Internal Revenue Service simultaneously appeared at my apartment in Manhattan and Tom Bolan's house in Queens. Since they arrived during working hours, neither Tom nor I was at home. At my apartment it fell to my mother to open the letter. The letters were identical. They announced that criminal prosecution of us and several of our associates was being recommended by the Special Squad, and five different "offenses" were cited. (One was more ludicrous than the next, but that

didn't help the shattered morale of my mother.) One would
have thought that even Internal Revenue could have been
decent enough to send such poisonous letters to our office
instead of our homes—and after years of intercepting our
mail they certainly knew our office address.

One of the "criminal" charges was for deducting an embezzlement loss of some money, but in this instance not
only was the money actually embezzled, but the culprits were
caught and sent to jail by District Attorney Hogan! Then,
there was a claim that we had an interest in one of Floyd
Patterson's companies—Floyd Patterson Enterprises—when
a decree by the state attorney general had established that
we did not. The other charges were equally absurd. Fortunately, Internal Revenue provides a review system, and
when the charges were reviewed by the Office of the Regional Counsel of Internal Revenue (Morgenthau actually
withheld some files from the reviewing group because he
resented the review), each and every one of the five charges
was summarily dismissed as being completely unfounded
and unsupported by the facts. Both the Treasury Department
and the Criminal Tax Division of the Justice Department
thereafter approved the dropping of charges. The result was
happy, but each of us and our included associates had to en-
gage counsel to appear before the regional office and spend
much time and money on investigation and compiling the
facts and documents to disprove the charges. We had to have
three lawyers and two accountants; the fees and expenses
of this senseless proceeding were about forty thousand dollars.

On September 25, 1962, the heavyweight title bout between Floyd Patterson and Sonny Liston was held in Chicago.
Championship Sports, Inc., a company owned mostly by Tom
Bolan and myself, promoted the fight. The fight didn't last
long, and the proceeds lasted an even shorter time. By the
time we reached a friend's home after the fight, we were

advised that all its proceeds—not only at the box office at Soldiers' Field but at theaters all around the country where the fight was shown on closed-circuit television—had been seized. This had been done at the instigation of then Attorney General Robert Kennedy. The excuse given for the seizure was that the "Government" was worried that Championship Sports might not pay taxes on their share (the taxes were not even due until the next year). And not only was Championship Sports' money seized, but the fighters', theater owners', and everyone else's. It was described editorially by the New York *Daily News* as one of the most high-handed examples of unbridled Big Brother power. Under tax procedures the funds were interpleaded into court, where we had to sue to get them back. In 1970 $435,000 is still held in court, and the case is working its way up the calendar. Our fees and expenses have been over $50,000. It is conceded that a substantial portion of the funds must be returned to us, but Morgenthau's office, which represented Internal Revenue in court, just wouldn't do it, and we have to wait our turn.

To raise the money required by all this legal activity, we had to work very hard, and we had to depend on the generosity of friends in making loans and extending credit. I am fortunate in that I am able to earn substantial amounts of money in my profession and have friends to help me when I have to take a partial leave of absence. At the time, although almost driven under financially, and knowing it would take me years to recover, I was still able to get by. My morale was kept up throughout by the realization of what people I was close to did to help me, not only in financial matters but also in every aspect of friendship. Once, when I was a little discouraged, I received a letter telling me to stop feeling sorry for myself and to count these blessings of friendship. It came from Barbara Walters, the pretty young lady whom I knew before she rose to her present unique position on the national television airwaves. But what about the plight of other targets of the Morgenthaus and Garrisons who do not have and cannot get the means to defend themselves adequately? So far, no way of recovering money or damages on an acquittal has been effectively pursued. William F. Buckley, Jr., made this point when he wrote:

> It happens that Roy Cohn is able and rich. But there are those who are neither, whose cases do not make the newspapers, but whose lives are wracked by the petty and major harassments of public officials who if they feel pangs of remorse at going after someone who is proved innocent, do not tend to exhibit them; and in any case, remorse is not accepted by banks as legal tender.

Buckley could well have had in mind the case of one of his secretaries' father. A prominent lawyer, legal scholar, and teacher—and very much a conservative—he was unjustly charged by Morgenthau with having criminally and willfully filed late tax returns. He was acquitted, but the intervening years between charge and acquittal cost him his livelihood, his health, and the ability to support his family.

During the six years, from 1963 to 1969 Morgenthau had seven assistant United States Attorneys who at one point or another were working full-time on me. A high percentage of his and his executive staff's time was devoted to his obsession with me. After my first indictment in 1963 I promptly made a statement concerning Morgenthau's personal animosity toward me. (Some people recalled my part in the hearings on the turnover of the United States occupation-currency plates to the Russians by Secretary Morgenthau. A lot didn't.) After that, Morgenthau adopted a policy of not coming near the courtroom during proceedings involving me. But to keep him *au courant,* he had stationed in the back of the courtroom during the two and one-half months of my trial his administrative assistant. During my first trial (and the preceding mistrial) he had a number of FBI agents working full-time on me. During and before the 1964 trial he had two S.E.C. staffers assigned full-time to him to work on me. For breathers in between my trials he used his special squad of ten Internal Revenue agents. We have estimated that he called before the grand jury over one thousand witnesses against me—each of whom had to be paid witness fees and transportation. Records mentioning me which he subpoenaed from all over the country would fill about eleven large rooms. He sent, on public funds, at least three people to Europe to investigate me and paid substantial sums to an undercover agent to go abroad and find out if I had a numbered Swiss bank account. (He could have called me and I would have given him the answer: No.)

The actual court proceedings and their cost tell only part of the story. For instance, our firm had some property damaged, the loss investigated and approved, and the check from the insurance company in the mail—eagerly awaited, as the money was needed for replacement. Perito, Morgenthau's principal assistant in charge of getting me at the time, suggested to the insurance company that they stop payment—which they did. He hinted to them that all our operations were illicit and that for some undefined reason we should not be paid for the loss under the policy. The check had already been sent out when Perito suggested a stop payment. When they found out I had papers ready to file in court seeking damages from Perito and the insurance company, the money was released.

On a less crucial level there was the young messenger working for us over the summer during his vacation from a parochial school. We needed some records returned that Perito had taken from us. Tom Bolan told one of our regular messengers to take a letter to Perito at the courthouse, requesting their return. The messenger was busy and asked the young messenger to take the letter to Perito. He did so. Perito descended upon him: Who gave you this letter?— When?—Where?—Don't tell me you don't know anything about it—You're interfering with a federal official in the performance of his duty—You can go to jail for this. Needless to say, the boy was badly shaken. I hope he didn't take his first experience with America's legal system as a representative of the system as a whole.

Morgenthau destroyed just about every banking relationship I had. He had banks furnishing copies of checks I issued on an almost daily basis. To avoid the nuisance, the banks would close the accounts. I had a loan at a bank secured by stock-market collateral. Morgenthau subpoenaed the president of the bank and directed him to produce the collateral. When he did, it was physically taken from him and impounded. We had to go to the Justice Department in Washington to get it back.

Young lawyers working for my law firm were directly told that if they continued with us, they would be prosecuted or named as conspirators. Girls I had gone out with were called to the courthouse and asked who we would see socially and what was discussed.

The mail interception caused such an upheaval that following Judge Dawson's admonition, one would think that Morgenthau and Internal Revenue would have learned enough to stop at least this tactic. But in the fall of 1966, two years later, I was deluged with phone calls—from my rabbi, the charge department at Saks Fifth Avenue, clients, personal friends. They were all to the same effect. Each one—and some three hundred others—had received a questionnaire from Internal Revenue announcing that I was under investigation and that they were seeking details about all financial transactions with me over a period of many years. I don't think that two people out of the three hundred had ever had any relevant financial transactions with me.

After recovering from the sense of outrage at such a letter being sent to the people such as my rabbi and personal friends (there was one good result: I received a call from a girl I had wanted to get in touch with but whose address I had lost), we tried to figure out how these particular people were selected as recipients of the Internal Revenue letter. We were stumped. Then, one morning, one of the lawyers in our office named Robert Cohen came in to say that one of the IRS letters about me had been received by a classmate of his who was serving overseas with the armed forces. Bob figured out that the last he had heard from his friend was about two years before, when the friend had written to Bob at the office to thank him for a wedding gift. From this we deduced that the IRS list was made up from names and addresses they had obtained by intercepting our office mail at the time of the trial and that Robert Cohen's army buddy got on the list because of the similarity of our names.

The story broke on the front page of *The New York Times,* and there was another outcry. Subsequent congressional hearings established that mail interception by the Post Office Department was widespread and carried out indiscriminately at the request of other agencies.

As painful as it is to know that your mail is being funneled into the hands of people like Morgenthau and that your friends are being told you're under investigation, it is equally trying to know that strangers you speak to—and prospective clients—might have been hired to tape what you say.

Jerry Allen, on the staff of a Wall Street stock-brokerage firm, was having difficulties with Morgenthau's office. They were threatening to indict him concerning some stock issue, although his involvement was at worst minor. Allen was brought in for questioning. Discussions concerning his possible "cooperation" with Morgenthau's office ensued. He was asked if perchance he knew me. He said that he did. (Actually, I did not even remember him, although he recalls that a number of years earlier he was with a group of people that came to see me about the purchase of a company.) They asked if he could furnish any information against me. Of course, he could not.

But another idea germinated. Could he get to see me again? He thought he could. Would he "go along" with wearing a concealed recorder when he saw me? He thought he would. And would he try to get me implicated in some illegal stock transaction during the taped conversation? Seeing his way out of being indicted himself, Allen agreed. In the days before we met, Morgenthau's staff kept pressuring him: When was he going to make contact "with the lawyer on Madison Avenue"? He finally called me, and we made an appointment. Maybe it was the nervousness in his voice, maybe it was a sixth sense, but when he arrived with one of his partners, I decided not to see them alone, and I asked John Vassallo, a lawyer in our firm, to sit in. Allen acted rather strangely and kept trying to get me to talk about some stock deal concerning shares I owned in a company. I told him I had no interest.

As it turned out, Allen had not followed instructions about having himself electronically equipped. He was beginning to find the whole thing distasteful. Instead, he taped some phone conversations between himself and members of Morgenthau's staff. After my indictment and my detailing some of the methods Morgenthau was using, Allen came to see me and told me the story. He later told it in a sworn affidavit.

Around this time we received a letter from Mannie Pollack, an inmate confined to state prison. He asked to be visited, and I sent one of the young lawyers from the office to see him. He wanted legal advice and representation in certain civil matters. In the course of the discussion he mentioned that he had been propositioned by Morgenthau's office to try to trap me. Pollack had been in jail in New Jersey at a time when Morgenthau charged the warden with some improprieties (under federal law the warden in New Jersey was prosecuted in the Southern District of New York). Pollack became a witness for Morgenthau against the warden and testified under the United States Attorney's auspices as a prosecution witness at the warden's trial.

Pollack got in trouble again with the state authorities. He went to Morgenthau's office to ask them to intercede. But what could he do for them? Well, for openers, did he know me? From that question on, there developed a wild-goose chase, in which it was impossible to tell who was conning whom more, Pollack or Morgenthau's staff. Pollack said that of course he knew me. He didn't. He then elaborated on our nonexistent relationship. He was propositioned to be electronically wired and sent to have an incriminating discussion with me—the same deal as with Allen. Pollack relates that he was actually shown a diagrammed layout of my office and was given a "briefcase" containing electronic recording devices.

Since Pollack was in a state jail, some method had to be found to get him to Morgenthau's office to perfect plans. Perito unhesitatingly swore out a false affidavit saying Pollack's presence was required before the grand jury in some spurious matter. It was all a ruse to get him to Perito's office. Pollack was never put before the grand jury, but he was brought to Perito's office on that writ some twenty-eight times. One day, while down on the phony writ, Perito actually let Pollack go home, ostensibly to look for something. Pollack had a pleasant day out of jail phoning his friends. Perito told Pollack to get as his lawyer a former colleague of Perito's. This was another subterfuge: The lawyer was never paid a dime's fee; he was put in there to sit on top of Pollack.

Well, Morgenthau's office did not deliver sufficiently for Pollack on his state-court matter, and he became angry. That is when he told us the story. We checked out his information, found proof of the phony writ, and got affidavits from him. When we filed the affidavits, Morgenthau's office put in reply affidavits calling Pollack every name in the book, one of the minor ones being that he was a notorious liar. But as Sidney Zion pointed out in *The New York Times,* Morgenthau's office had but recently vouched for Pollack's credibility by using him as a prosecution witness against the warden and represented to that jury that Pollack was a truthful man.

It is a relatively easy matter for the Government (or, for that matter, private individuals) to use electronic devices and recording equipment. The varieties of equipment are extensive. To record a conversation, one can conceal a tape recorder in a briefcase. But this method has given way to much more sophisticated devices such as miniature recorders concealed in a "wristwatch" or "tie clip." Investigations have shown that these devices have been in widespread use, particularly by the Internal Revenue Service.

Many people were outraged when the Judiciary Subcommittee headed by Senator Edward V. Long, of Missouri, exposed the frequent use of these devices by IRS, even to the point where devices were concealed behind pictures and the American flag in IRS conference rooms to which a taxpayer had been summoned. This meant IRS would pick up a conversation between the taxpayer and his own lawyer who accompanied him to the conference. Long's effective work and that of Bernard Fensterwald, the committee's counsel, rubbed too many of the high-up users of these Gestapo methods the wrong way, resulting in a Bobby Kennedy–inspired article in *Life* against Long, written by William Lambert and used successfully against Long in his Senate primary fight in Missouri.

Late in 1970, in New York Federal Court before Judge Edmund Palmieri, an Internal Revenue Agent named Lawrence Ruggiero told about how he had been equipped for a conference with an unsuspecting taxpayer and his tax adviser:

Q. How was this actually attached to you, sir?
A. This transmitter was a small one, and it was placed in an athletic supporter which I wore, and the microphone would then be put up along my chest and would be taped to my chest.
Q. And about how big was the transmitter?
A. The transmitter was about the size of a pack of cigarettes and slightly thinner in width, but about the size of a pack of cigarettes and a little more square.

Although the bugging incidents with Allen and Pollack did not invade my personal life, wiretapping did. The night before Carol Horn was to testify before my 1968 grand jury, we spoke at length on the telephone. The next day the assistant district attorney was sufficiently indiscreet as to reveal exactly what Carol and I had discussed. Is there anyone who would not object to having private phone conversations exposed to the United States Attorney's office?

The Federal Communications Act has specifically made wiretapping illegal. For years the Supreme Court has forbidden the use in federal prosecutions not only of wire taps themselves but of any information obtained as a result of having used them. Such indirect information was branded the "fruit of a poisonous tree" by the Supreme Court in the Nardone case.

State-authorized wiretapping must be authorized by court order, but the obtaining of court approval is often a meaningless formality. The state official draws up a secret affidavit, which the judge puts in a safe along with the order authorizing the wiretap. There have probably been thousands of these signed.

Wiretapping has been widespread, both officially and unofficially. Many liberal power dusters were quite shaken up with the recent disclosure that Attorney General Kennedy had a wiretap on Martin Luther King, Jr. And, even then, it was a poorly kept secret that Bobby ran an "unofficial" wiretap operation, headed by one of his trusted Washington associates. Apparently, when liberals thought his targets were only people like Jimmy Hoffa, such tactics were palatable.

Private wiretapping, strictly illegal under both state and federal laws, is often used in matrimonial cases, business disputes, political contests, and so forth. Surprisingly enough, our ubiquitous friend, Mr. Morgenthau, the darling of such militant antiwiretappers as James Wechsler, turns out to have been a wiretapper of no small consequence himself when he was in private practice. A client of his was involved is highly competitive proceedings before the Federal Power Commission, and Morgenthau secretly hired a wiretapper who went in on the lines of the competitor and certain public officials. Payments for the illegal operation were carefully camouflaged by our champion of civil rights.

It is a relatively easy proposition to wiretap privately. An investigator who knows telephone lines and how they work locates the proper pair along the line and places an intercepting device on the wire. The old days of the "receiving station," where the tappers sit in a room surrounded by equipment and listen to the results, are passé. The tapped conversations can now be automatically recorded or listened to in a moving automobile.

It may surprise some people that I oppose the use of wiretapping, bugging, and mail interception. This is not a newly found position, based upon a naturally justifiable reaction to having been a victim of their use. I do not deny their efficacy in detecting crime. But these methods are too gross and basic an invasion of privacy and civil rights to make them justifiable. It's too high a price to pay for detecting crime. I came to this conclusion a great many years ago. As a federal prosecutor over twenty years ago, right after I got out of law school, I never ordered or utilized wiretapping, bugging, or mail interception. Yet I was not regarded as soft, and for whatever it might prove, I never lost any of the dozens of cases I prosecuted. I believe the law can be effectively enforced without the use of these devices.

Furthermore, in the cases against me no one was sent to jail as a result of such devices, whereas many criminals were set free as a result of shady deals.

I believe that if the rights of one man are threatened, the rights of all men are. In this sense the public suffered. The public also suffered by the fact that no less than ten persons went unpunished just by agreeing to play Morgenthau's game:

> Samuel Garfield, ex-convict, pleaded guilty to stock swindling ....suspended sentence
> Sidney Barkley, ex-convict, pleaded guilty to stock swindling ....suspended sentence
> Allard Roen, Las Vegas kingpin, pleaded guilty to stock swindling ....suspended sentence
> Allen K. Swann, pleaded guilty to stock swindling ....suspended sentence
> Morton Weinberg, confessed conspirator in bribery ....not indicted
> Bernard Patrusky, confessed perjurer and blackmailer ....not indicted
> Lawrence Weisman, confessed bribe participant ....not prosecuted, but given formal immunity
> Bernard Reicher, pleaded guilty to grand larceny and perjury indictment in 1967 ....not sentenced (as of 1971)
> Victor Muscat, pleaded guilty to felonies of filing false statements with the S.E.C. in 1969 ......not sentenced (as of 1971)
> Edward Krock, pleaded guilty to felonies of false statement to Government in 1969 ....not sentenced (as of 1971)

The price of injustice is high indeed.

IX

Trial by *Life*

BEFORE EACH OF my trials *Life* magazine, working in league with Morgenthau, flooded the district with an article, clearly designed to create irremediable prejudice against me. The authors of the first article were William Lambert and Keith Wheeler. Lambert, who usually spoke for Bobby Kennedy and Morgenthau, also wrote the second one.

The first—"Roy Cohn: Is He a Liar under Oath?"—hit the stands one month after my first indictment. By combining outright falsehood with deceptive innuendo the article painted me as a conniving perjurer. It tried to support, point by point, the charges in my indictment and added many "facts" and charges against me that were not even mentioned in it. Liberal writer Tom Morgan described the article as yellow journalism.

It was obvious to us from the outset that the article, geared to prejudice public opinion—and prospective jurors —against me, had as its godfathers Roberts Kennedy and Morgenthau and William Mulligan, the lawyer for Garfield, Roen, and Swann, who were to be witnesses against me at the trial in return for their own freedom. But our belief that they had masterminded the article was as strong as our doubt that we could ever prove it. If we could, we would have had a strong basis for having the indictment dismissed on the ground that the Justice Department had deliberately created prejudicial publicity about a defendant awaiting trial.

The article's allusions to the unpublished "inside" story of the case, the publication of facts not in the indictment, and the attempt to argue my guilt all added up, in our eyes, to the strongest case of circumstantial evidence that the prosecution had inspired and helped with the article. But when we made a motion for dismissal, Judge Dawson denied us a hearing on the grounds that we had no actual proof that any Government officials were involved.

Our interest in the *Life* article heightened after the spring mistrial. During the trial we had found that some of the prosecution-witness testimony at the trial itself contradicted what *Life* had predicted these witnesses would say. This indicated that they had made prior inconsistent statements to which *Life* had had access and which we could use to cross-examine them at the retrial. To try to get the full story, we served a subpoena on the Time-Life Corporation for its files on the article about me. We arranged for Tom Bolan to examine the files in their counsel's office. Late one afternoon he went to the offices of *Life*'s Wall Street law firm. Tom said he'd call when he had looked at the file. Hours went by and no word. I skipped dinner and waited at the office, wondering why I hadn't heard from Tom.

About 9 P.M. the night line on my desk rang shrilly through the empty office. "Wait for me. I'll be there in twenty minutes. I can't talk from here." When Tom arrived, I saw a look of controlled enthusiasm on his face. He walked in and put down his briefcase. "You won't believe it," he said. "Not only do we have proof that the Justice Department from Bobby on down collaborated on the article, but it was actually proofread and changed by Mulligan. The lawyer for prospective witnesses and the prosecution masterminding a smear job against a defendant awaiting trial!

"And I've saved the biggest news for last. I don't know how it happened, or why, but mixed in with the papers in your file I found a series of secret memos on the Jimmy Hoffa case. They show that Bobby Kennedy personally engineered a vicious article against Hoffa while he was awaiting trial and literally begged *Life* to publish it."

Tom, proficient at shorthand, sat down, and characters skimmed across the paper that the next day became an affidavit in support of a new motion:

> The proof, unavailable before Judge Dawson, is now at hand as a result of the fact that *Life* magazine only this week complied with a defense subpoena for its files. . . . Mr. Mulligan's testimony, and the documents he is able to produce, will conclusively demonstrate that prosecution witnesses Garfield and Roen gave or authorized their counsel to give to *Life* magazine a story quite at variance from the one told by them at this trial.
>
> For example, on page 102 of the *Life* magazine article, it is alleged that in August, 1959, there was a meeting in New York between Government witnesses Swann, Garfield, Roen, and Barkley. This statement, along with the entire *Life* article, was proofread and corrected by Mr. Mulligan prior to publication. Nevertheless, at the prior trial of this indictment, it was consistently denied that Mr. Roen was in New York during the period in question.
>
> Defendants should be entitled to utilize Mr. Mulligan's testimony and documents, attributable to and disclosed in behalf of the Government witnesses, to show that on a prior occasion they made statements concerning this case inconsistent with their present trial testimony.
>
> By way of proof that Mr. Mulligan contributed to the composition of the *Life* magazine article in question, I an-

nex as Exhibit B hereto, an office memorandum written by the coauthor of the *Life* article, which reads as follows: "These are the suggested revisions given me by Mulligan, in his own handwriting, clipped to the sheets which he proposes revising."

Further, the files of *Life* magazine have been inspected by me and conclusively demonstrate that the authors of the article in question conferred in the preparation of the article with several officials of the U.S. Attorney's office and with Mr. Ed Guthman, an aide to the Attorney General of the United States, Mr. Herbert Miller, chief of the Criminal Division of the Department of Justice, and the Attorney General of the United States, Mr. Robert F. Kennedy.

Thus, the chief of the Criminal Division of the Department of Justice stated to the *Life* magazine people: "Evidence was developed that there had been an effort to bribe public officials—namely Morton Robson, the assistant U.S. Attorney named in the indictment."

As this court is well aware, no such charge is made in the indictment.

The shocking fact is that there is good reason to believe that the *Life* magazine story had its genesis in the office of the Attorney General himself. I attach hereto a copy of a telegram sent from *Life*'s Washington office (Exhibit C) as long ago as May 2, 1962, to *Life* Editor Edward K. Thompson, arranging a meeting for Mr. Thompson with the Attorney General. This telegram was found in the "Roy Cohn" file at *Life* magazine.

Such activity on the part of the Department of Justice as presently constituted appears to be but a common course of conduct. Thus, the department has inspired and arranged for national publicity concerning persons under investigation or indictment. This can only be described as an attempt to establish guilt by prearrangement.

As proof hereof, I annex hereto, as Exhibits D and E, from the "Cohn files" turned over to us by *Life* magazine, a personal and confidential memorandum and letter from

the Washington bureau of *Life* to Editor Thompson re-
lating to the "cloak and dagger" methods by which the
Attorney General himself inspired such an inflammatory
and prejudicial article in *Life* magazine concerning
another man under investigation by the grand jury and
who, with Mr. Cohn, is commonly known to be at the
head of the Attorney General's "list"—James R. Hoffa.

The Attorney General, apparently concerned with the
propriety of his extrajudicial conduct in this regard, instructed the people at *Life* not to handle this matter "by
phone." He apparently entertained the notion that the U.S.
mails were more private than telephones. Perhaps they
were insofar as he was concerned, but even this freedom
of privacy was not afforded the defendants in this case.
Their mail was intercepted by the Department of Justice.

The memo in question, from Edward Thompson, of *Life,*
dated March 6, 1961, says:

Last Saturday I got a phone call from Bob Kennedy asking if I could drop whatever I was doing and come to his
office. I did, and when I got there he closed the door and
told me the following: In a back room was a high official
of the Teamsters, a man who had been privy to the inner
workings of the organization since 1953. He was particularly knowledgeable about Hoffa. This official is honest,
said Kennedy, and also quite an idealist. The man had been
working directly with Kennedy and in secret for the last
two years. He was now so disillusioned and disgusted with
the corruption he saw around him, particularly as concerns Hoffa, that he has just about decided to make a public break with the union. Kennedy said he has suggested
to this man that he make his break via an article in *Life*
in the form of a personal exposé of Hoffa. Kennedy asked
my personal word that for the moment only you and I
would know of this matter. Kennedy feels, perhaps melo-
dramatically, perhaps not, that the man's life would be in

danger if word leaked out of his intentions. I told the Attorney General that if you were interested in this man's story, and if we did go ahead, more and more people at *Life* would have to become involved. Kennedy understood this, but pointed out that if we are not interested, then only two people, as he put it, that he personally knows and trusts, will have had to know about it. I gave my word. He also asked that if we do want to go ahead, or at least look into the possibilities, in other words when we have to pass the point of only you and I being involved, we let him know first. I said we would.

Of course this guy has an ax to grind and so, as you of course know, does Bobby Kennedy (see the Kennedy-Hoffa cartoon in yesterday's News of the Week in Review section of the *Times*).

Anyway, that's the story. If you'd like to have Graves or one of the text-writers go into this more deeply with Baron, still just on an exploratory basis, I'm sure Kennedy and Baron will buy that.

Incidentally, since I gave the assurance I wouldn't handle any of this by phone, except in the most general way, could you respond on paper. Please be sure the envelope is plainly marked "P. & C."

As shocking as was the way the article about me was written, the blatancy of the article's lies was even more so. I had recommended New York attorney Murray Gottesman to Garfield. *Life*'s premise was that I didn't know Gottesman but dug him up from the Republican leadership to fix Garfield's case, and this was my "association" with Murray Gottesman. The fact is that Gottesman and I had a number of very apparent professional associations with each other over the years, details of which *Life* could have easily discovered by a minimum of research or by asking.

Another lie was that "according to the indictment, it was Robson whom Gottesman contacted." The indictment contained no such statement. The motive for this lie is found in *Life*'s preceding sentence: "In August, 1959, Morton S. Robson, who had a reputation as an effective prosecutor, was Chief Assistant U.S. Attorney in the Southern District of New York and naturally exercised certain authority in any proceedings which might arise in the United Dye case." But as Hazard Gillespie testified, Robson exercised no authority in the United Dye case.

Life turned to charges that I attempted "to put the squeeze on Garfield and Roen" and that this was done through Moe Dalitz, one of Roen's partners in the Desert Inn in Las Vegas. *Life* commented that I "could scarcely have chosen a more appropriate vise than Dalitz" and went on to detail a seemingly close relationship between Dalitz and me. They relied on the fact that we had both invested in a private hospital and were socially friendly. They concealed the public fact that there were many investors in the hospital from all over the country, that my investment was small, and that I had sold it before Dalitz was to be my "vise." Even staler news was the social relationship: My friend had been Mrs. Dalitz, who had divorced Dalitz some time before the case. I was high on his private-enemy list because of my regard for his former wife. Indeed, a prosecution witness quoted Dalitz as saying that he "would spend five years in jail to put Roy Cohn there for one day."

The big thrust of the *Life* article was in its handling of the charge that I had lied in saying I had attended a meeting at the Pierre Hotel in August, 1959, with Garfield, Swann, and Gottesman. Beginning on this point, *Life* said, "But the Cohn indictment bears down most severely" on my testimony that there had been such a meeting. They say I was inaccurate in my physical description of Swann and that it therefore follows that I had never met him. They suggested that by inventing such a meeting I was saying that my involvement with Garfield, Swann, Roen, and Barkley was to give legitimate legal advice, rather than to fix the case in some way.

Life argues that because of my sinister dealings with these people, "it was necessary to him to shape that record to his favor," and thus the meeting was invented. And to "prove" the meeting was an invention, *Life* devoted considerable space to the fact that before the grand jury in April, 1963, I had given an imperfect physical description of Swann.

I had met Swann once in my life—in August, 1959. I was questioned about it four years later—April, 1963. I was asked to describe him, and I recalled that he was gray-haired and long-winded. When pressed about his height, I replied that I did not recall having seen him standing up and did not know how tall he was. Morgenthau's assistant, Walpin, kept pushing me on this point, and I said that since his height didn't make an impression on me, my guess would be that he was probably of average height. *Life* described the questioning:

> U.S. Attorney Gerald Walpin kept returning again and again to Cohn's recollection of Swann's height. When first asked, Cohn's answer was, "I would say his height was— I don't think he was very short, or very tall—I'd say average, or above average. I don't know. I just don't."
>
> Walpin, evidently unsatisfied, pursued the question. He asked Cohn to set forth his definition of "average." He asked Cohn how tall he himself was and, when Cohn replied, "Five-eight," he wanted to know whether Cohn considered that average. Cohn replied, "I would say average to short—on the short side." Walpin then volunteered that he himself was 5 feet 4½, and what did Cohn think of that. "I'd consider you on the short side. I'd probably consider myself on the short side a little," Cohn answered.

The issue was absurd. Three facts should have suggested to Walpin that he was on the wrong track in believing that the meeting had never taken place: (1) Knowing Garfield and Swann had made deals against me with Morgenthau, why would I invent a meeting and place two hostile witnesses there who would surely contradict me? (2) If I were telling a carefully planned lie about having been at a meeting with Swann, it would have been a cinch for me to get an accurate and detailed description of him. (3) My description of Swann was as reasonably accurate as could have been expected of anyone describing someone he had met only once four years before—I recalled his gray hair and his long-windedness. As for his height, had I seen him standing up, I might have remembered it, though probably I would not have.

Life took great pains to demonstrate that I must have been lying, not only because Swann was over six feet tall but also because he spoke with an Oklahoma accent, which, of course, any truthful person would clearly recall four years later. Only a liar wouldn't immediately be able to identify an Oklahoma accent heard for half an hour four years before. *Life* put it this way:

> Well, then, whatever the reach and span of Cohn's memory, Allen K. Swann, in full, roaring life size, is a man of quite remarkable appearance and mannerism. He is a big man physically, broad of shoulder and powerful of hand, lean and rangy and more than 6 feet tall. Although he is now 71 years old (67 at the time Cohn claims to have met him), he still has a head of sandy gray hair. His visage is distinctive, he has a jutting jaw and a general appearance of flatness and strength which, moreover, is somehow emphasized by horn-rimmed spectacles with thick lenses. He is quite deaf and wears a hearing aid attached to his spectacle frames. And, perhaps because of his deafness, he speaks in a loud, booming voice which still carries the accents of Oklahoma where he was born. In all, he's a very memorable man.

Then came the crusher. To prove I couldn't have forgotten

Swann's height, *Life* published a full-page picture of him, standing on a curb looking so tall he had to stoop over slightly to avoid hitting the sky. And to cement the point, *Life* posed him holding an open umbrella over his head to create an illusion that would dwarf Wilt Chamberlain into insignificance.

Interestingly, *Life*'s premise that if Swann and I had ever met, it would have been unforgettable and indelibly engraved upon both of our minds exploded seconds after my lawyer, Frank Raichle, began cross-examining Swann at the retrial in 1964. At the first trial, only ninety days earlier, Henry K. Chapman, representing Gottesman, had cross-examined Swann first, and Raichle, representing me, second. At the retrial we reversed the order, and Raichle cross-examined before Chapman. Swann had been expecting Chapman first, and when Raichle stood up, Swann mistook him for Chapman, even though Swann had been cross-examined by Raichle at length only weeks before! Here was the man swearing under oath he would have remembered talking to me in a group of four people for half an hour some five years ago, unable to recognize his cross-examiner from the same season. The colloquy went:

> RAICHLE: Now, Mr. Swann, you were indicted in 1960 in an indictment containing how many counts?
>
> SWANN: I don't remember, Mr. Chapman.
>
> THE COURT: This is Mr. Raichle, Mr. Swann.
>
> SWANN: I mean Mr. Raichle. Are you Mr. Raichle? I thought you were Mr. Chapman.
>
> RAICHLE: You have the same difficulty remembering me, whom you saw at the last trial, that you do Mr. Gottesman and Mr. Cohn at the Pierre Hotel; is that right?

Tom Bolan wrote a detailed letter to *Life* refuting the article. *Life* truncated his letter and published the remaining few paragraphs in the letters column.

After the trial we faced the question of whether or not to sue for libel. This is always a difficult decision. Among the considerations in favor of suing are: (1) If you don't, some people regard the failure to do so as an admission of the truth of the published statements. (2) When one is libeled, particularly for commercial purposes, why let the people responsible get away with it? (3) Why not get back some of the money their libelous statements have cost you in loss of business, reputation, and so on?

Among the factors against suing are: (1) There is a legal difficulty, particularly for a public figure, in view of Supreme Court decisions giving great leeway to statements about people in public life under the umbrella of freedom of the press and fair comment. (2) The expense of obtaining counsel, stenographic transcripts, research, investigation, etc., can be substantial. (3) Since a libel suit is predicated on your good reputation, the publication you sue can go into your activities in some depth in an effort to show that you did not have a sufficiently good reputation that could be libeled.

Many libel suits are settled before trial, as the risk to the publication being sued is great. In addition to actual damages the jury may award punitive damages in a high amount to punish the libeling publication. The libel actions by Coaches Wally Butts and Paul Bryant against the *Saturday Evening Post* were successful to the tune of, in Butts's case, $3 million in punitive damages and $60,000 actual damages (reduced to $460,000 on appeal) and in Bryant's case a tax-free $300,000, payments that undoubtedly contributed to that magazine's demise. We settled a libel action against Time-Life concerning an article they had run in *Sports Illustrated* about a client of ours, Julius November, who was the attorney for heavyweight champion Floyd Patterson. We had to show that the statements were not legally within the freedom-of-press and fair-comment doctrines. The libel complaint we filed in the November case was dismissed by the appellate division, the intermediate appellate court in New York. I argued the final appeal before the Court of Appeals in Albany, and the complaint was reinstated by a divided court. Settlement followed.

Senator Barry Goldwater mounted a successful libel challenge against Ralph Ginzberg, the pornographer, in federal court. One of Ginzberg's publications had concluded that Goldwater was unbalanced. Goldwater showed characteristic courage by suing in liberal New York City, and he won a unanimous jury verdict, which was affirmed on appeal.

We weighed all the factors in my situation after I was acquitted. The same people who had advised me not to make public the facts about Morgenthau's animosity because I might further antagonize him, now counseled me not to sue *Life*. "Don't remind people" and "Leave well enough alone" were the comments. Tom Bolan said: "The article was a dishonest, contrived piece of filthy journalism, designed to convict you before trial. You have the capacity to fight. If you don't, what chance is there for less fortunate victims of something like this?" I decided to sue.

Emile Zola Berman, nicknamed "Zuke," is the bold, thorough lawyer who went from fame within legal circles for his unvarying success in negligence cases to national renown for his defense of Marine Sergeant McKeon. Zuke and his partner, Harold Frost, had long been good friends of mine, and I asked Zuke to represent me. We filed the necessary papers. Then the series of Supreme Court decisions liberalizing what could be written about public figures appeared, and we decided to see what effect they had on other cases before proceeding. "If only *Life* would do another smear article on you. Then we could prove actual malice toward you—which I know they have—and we'd be in perfect shape," Zuke told me one day in 1968. Neither of us then knew that the same magazine, one of the same authors, William Lambert, and the same planter of poisoned pretrial apples, Morgenthau, were soon to oblige.

In the early summer of 1969 I received two separate reports that Lambert, still stinging from my acquittal, was on the hustings again. I was told that now that a firm date for my new trial had been set for September, he and Morgenthau were determined to try again to do me in by a pretrial article geared to prejudice the public against me as much as possible.

Tom Bolan was with his family in California, and I was there spending a weekend with my favorite hippie friend, Brian Butler, the son of Paul Butler, the late chairman of the Democratic National Committee. Tom came to Brian's Malibu cottage, and I told him what I had learned of *Life*'s plans. "They can't be that dumb," was his reaction, "but just in case, I recommend that you put them on immediate written notice." In the name of my law firm, Saxe, Bacon & Bolan, I dictated and sent the following letter to *Life* that day:

> We are advised that *Life* is planning publication of an article containing prejudicial and libelous references to Roy M. Cohn prior to his forthcoming trial.
>
> Mr. Cohn was acquitted on all ten counts of previous charges initiated by the same prosecutor, Mr. Morgenthau, whose six-year-long personal vendetta against Mr. Cohn is widely known. Prior to that trial, *Life* published an article containing similarly libelous and damaging statements about Mr. Cohn, including alleged points in support of the Morgenthau charges, which points were unanimously rejected by the jury. A suit by Mr. Cohn based upon that article is pending. This is to advise that publication of another article concerning Mr. Cohn as the next trial approaches will be a clear demonstration of actual malice on *Life*'s part, and will be so treated legally.

In addition, as a matter of common fairness, it is respectfully submitted that *Life* might consider the spirit of the order entered by Federal Judge Wyatt to the effect that the issues be left to the jury without pre-trial publicity which might affect the outcome. Publication of an article by you would make this difficult at best, and we ask your consideration in this regard.

Late in August similar reports reached Judge Wyatt and he wrote to Hedley Donovan, *Life* editor-in-chief:

On September 23 next, the trial is scheduled to begin before a jury and me of an indictment (69 Cr. 55) in which Roy M. Cohn and three others are named as defendants.

It has come to my attention that there are persistent rumors, especially in the newspaper fraternity, that *Life* magazine is shortly to feature an article or articles about Mr. Cohn. If such rumors have no foundation in fact, there is no problem.

If, however, *Life* should publish an article about Mr. Cohn before or during the trial, there would be a serious problem. Any such article before the trial might affect the ability of our Court to select the fairest jury possible and any such article after the selection of a jury might affect the ability of the jury to act as impartially as possible.

The public interest as well as that of the defendants lies in securing the fairest trial possible.

I address you, therefore, to express the hope that, if *Life* is going to publish some article about Mr. Cohn, you can make publication at a time after the trial has been completed.

This matter is in my view urgent and important and if it cannot receive your personal attention, it will be appreciated if you will place it before the proper person for consideration.

Yet before the 1969 trial, *Life* abruptly overrode the judge's request and went right to it again. This article had more political implications and less about the case itself—although there was enough of that, too—than the previous one.

A friend of mine connected with *Life* told me he would have an advance copy of the magazine the Saturday before the Tuesday it would be on the stands. This was over the Labor Day weekend. I was sailing off Cape Cod that hot Saturday afternoon with Carol Horn and Si Newhouse. When we had put into port, I went to a phone booth and called my friend. "How bad is it?" I asked. His reply: "The pictures of you are really great—the best I've ever seen." That answered my question. Since I am not planning a movie career, the excellence of the pictures was small consolation—but some consolation, as I almost invariably photograph very poorly (something I discovered was not the fault of the photographers when I looked in the mirror one day).

I asked him to summarize the content. "Okay," he said. "It's a smear. You're presented as someone trying desperately to escape being brought to justice by that champion of the people, Bob Morgenthau. It very cleverly tries to embarrass all of your friends in politics and the press by implying that you buy them off to protect you. You won't believe this part, but it opens up by implying that Nixon fired Manny Cohen, the chairman of the S.E.C., and is trying to fire Morgenthau, to repay you for contributions and favors you did for him during the campaign."

I was almost speechless. "They must be nuts," I said. "Do they actually expect people to believe that were it not for me, Nixon would have been the first President in history to keep appointive heads of agencies from the administration he beat in the election?"

"Don't argue with *me*," my friend continued. "I'm only telling you what it says. My wife said just about the only thing you didn't get blamed for was the replacement of the Secretary of State."

"What else?" I asked him.

"Well," he said, "the point of it is obviously to get your friends to desert you and to scare Nixon into keeping Morgenthau—it reads like an obvious Morgenthau plant, just like the last. And they imply that Morgenthau's really got you this time and that you're going to be convicted."

On my return to the city Sunday night I read the article.

My friend's summary was accurate. And the pictures were good. The article was headlined:

His friends and influence can take care
of almost anything—except perhaps a trial
THAT HOTSHOT ONE-MAN ROY COHN LOBBY
by William Lambert

The opening paragraphs go right into the Nixon theme:

Last October 8, as the polls showed Richard Nixon running substantially ahead in the campaign for the Presidency, Roy Cohn moved to lend a hand. With his law associate, Thomas Bolan, he convened a luncheon meeting of perhaps a dozen wealthy New Yorkers at the quietly genteel Lotos Club in Manhattan's East 60s. Prominent among those present were two leading Nixon campaigners: chief fund-raiser Maurice Stans, who would become Nixon's Secretary of Commerce, and Louis Nichols, a former assistant director of the FBI and, until late last year, executive vice president of Schenley Industries.

Cohn, a registered Democrat, was blunt about his interest in the campaign. He had been having a lot of legal troubles and court actions. What, he asked the visitors, would a Nixon administration do about his two chief tormentors, Chairman Manuel Cohen of the Securities and Exchange Commission, and Robert Morgenthau, U.S. Attorney for the southern district of New York? Both Nichols and Stans disclaim any recollection of the discussion, but others present recall that their response was forthright: Nichols guaranteed that Morgenthau would be replaced, and Stans gave assurance that a way could be found to force Cohen to resign. The luncheon group dispersed after signing checks and pledges to the Nixon-Agnew campaign totaling more than $40,000. Seven months ago, Hamer H. Budge replaced Cohen as head of the SEC. Morgenthau is still U.S. Attorney in New York City, but rumors of his imminent replacement have recurrently appeared in the press.

The next paragraph announced that my contribution was nine thousand dollars. This was one of the many outright lies in the article. In the first place, I contributed not a penny to the Nixon campaign. And although I vote independently, as a registered, lifelong Democrat, I do not contribute to Republican campaigns. My presence was as a courtesy to my law associate, Tom Bolan, who was indeed a strong Nixon supporter, and who is one of the founders of the Conservative party in New York.

Beyond that, would readers actually believe that there was a relationship between the replacement of the head of S.E.C. by the new administration, which obviously replaced the head of every agency, and my insignificant support of Nixon?

The account of the luncheon was a lie, too. There was no such discussion. Just imagine Stans and Nichols getting up in front of a bunch of strangers and saying that if you contribute, we'll fire the head of S.E.C. and the U.S. Attorney. I knew immediately that the "source" of the fabricated version had to be Larry Weisman, Morgenthau's latest ally, who had been granted criminal immunity. Weisman was at the lunch with a friend of his, who incidentally welched on his pledged contribution. After the article, we spoke with everyone else present, and they, to a man, put the lie to Lambert's version. I told Nichols that the source had to be Weisman and his

friend. "I can't believe it," Nichols responded. "How could
Life base something this important on Weisman's word,
knowing that he was in a criminal immunity deal with Morgenthau and has the credibility of a Peking peach plea?"

At a later date we established as a fact that Weisman and
his friend were the only sources of the misinformation. The
lunch was actually a routine, small-scale fund-raising lunch
for a group of local Republican businessmen, none of whom
wanted anything or asked for anything, and who were far
more concerned with discussing foreign and domestic policy
than they were with Morgenthau and Mannie Cohen.

Another *Life* source made Weisman look like Diogenes by
comparison. A man who had been officially declared to be a
liar by a New York court contributed this story:

> One of Cohn's most powerful and oldest New York asso-
> ciates was the late Francis Cardinal Spellman, whose
> friendship derived from their mutual battles against
> communism. The cardinal's nephew, Ned Spellman, still
> is associated with various Cohn enterprises. When Spell-
> man's successor, Archbishop Terence Cooke, was invested
> as cardinal in Rome, Cohn turned up for the ceremonies.
> Uninvited, he also breezed into a dinner for the new car-
> dinal at a Rome hotel, said hello and left.

I can grin and bear it when called a thief and a liar, but
my mother would never have forgiven them for saying that
my manners were so bad that I went someplace "uninvited."
The formal invitations to the dinner to which *Life* said I
was "uninvited" will be produced at the libel trial. I use
"invitation" in the plural advisedly. I arrived in Rome late
and did not stay at the hotel at which I had expected to. Thus
the invitation to the dinner—which was far from private and
exclusive, as it included hundreds of New Yorkers who had
come to Rome on package tours—didn't catch up with us. A
new one was sent along, and the original arrived later. So

with two invitations to the dinner to which *Life* said I was
"uninvited," perhaps I can get double damages.

Not content with local New York liars for sources,
Life went to Chicago under the benign sponsorship of Victor
Muscat, who is awaiting sentence following a plea of guilty
to filing false statements with government agencies. I guess
Life thought he'd tell them the truth. The Chicago expedi-
tion elicited the support of the former president of a bank
controlled by clients of mine. He told *Life* a story about a
mortgage loan on a sailboat I sponsored to a corporation controlled by William F. Buckley, Jr.

Life reports that its local informant, the bank president at
that time, objected to the loan, "and the banker's obduracy
ulimately cost him his job." If *Life* had ascertained the
facts, they would have found that this martyr informant was
not fired, but promoted at the time, and left much later. He
went to work for another bank and lasted there only a very
short time. In any event the article concluded that Buckley
was a man of substantial wealth and that the loan was at
such high rates that he was being taken advantage of by
the bank. Naturally, it follows that because I arranged an
unfair loan, Buckley is grateful enough to write about me
favorably in his column. Perhaps sloppiness inevitably sets
in when a magazine deliberately sets out to do a hatchet job.

Switching back to the East Coast, *Life* came up with its
next episode of the Perils of Roy Cohn, this one involving
my friendship with Lou Nichols and his employment by
Schenley Industries after retiring from the FBI:

> When Nichols decided to retire from the FBI in 1957,
> Cohn set out to land him a job with Schenley. He had the
> willing support of another [Lewis S.] Rosenstiel [head of
> Schenley] friend, the late conservative columnist George
> Sokolsky, for whom Nichols represented 100% anti-Com-
> munist Americanism. At a social evening in August, 1967

[*sic*], Cohn and Sokolsky agreed to try to sell Nichols to
Rosenstiel as prime executive timber.

The next night they made their pitch to Rosenstiel.
Nichols, Cohn contended, was a genius, truly "one of the
greatest men in America," whereupon Rosenstiel
dispatched the Schenley private plane to Washington to
fly Nichols and his wife to a conference at Rosenstiel's
Greenwich, Conn. estate. Rosenstiel agreed to give Nichols
a 10-year contract at $100,000 a year, plus stock options,
in addition to arranging for the Schenleys to buy and furnish a Manhattan apartment for Nichols.

The account of Nichols's employment is a lie. As the article
subsequently revealed, however, such a "favor" done by me
for Nichols would supposedly account for his return favors
for me. Rosenstiel had not met him through me at all and
had himself offered Nichols the post on several prior occasions
without any prompting from me. *Life*'s source is once again
obvious. Rosenstiel lost his wife after a twenty-eight-year
idyllic marriage. In 1956 he had the misfortune to marry a
lady whom he later divorced in an acrimonious litigation.
In mid 1970 a jury not only awarded judgment against her
in a suit brought by a jeweler who accused her of having
stolen eighteen thousand dollars' worth of gems but also
slapped her with thirty thousand dollars in punitive damages. In February, 1971, she was indicted for perjury. As
Rosenstiel's lawyer, I inherited a high place on her enemy
list. So did Nichols, who caught on to her game early and
warned Rosenstiel. She was undoubtedly the source of this
particular group of lies; she had previously gone to Washington to try to get Drew Pearson to print them. At that point
her own lawyer, Louis Nizer, threw in the towel and stopped
representing her. But she became another member of the
parade of "reliable" confidential informants for Lambert
and *Life*.

The article attempted to prejudice my forthcoming trial

by focusing on two incidents. The first involved the transfer of three FBI agents who had given affidavits to Morgenthau's office in reply to the affidavit of Mannie Pollack, who was one of the people Morgenthau's office had propositioned to trap me into some deal or admission while he was electronically wired. *Life* suggests that Nichols engineered their transfer "to show his gratitude for Cohn's favors." The agents were apparently transferred for what *Life* concedes was their violation of strictly enforced Bureau rules. Their transfer meant absolutely nothing to me. Morgenthau's planted publicity about this incident in *Life* and elsewhere suggested that I had them spirited out of New York so they wouldn't be around to testify against me. Lambert must have been embarrassed when Morgenthau never called them at the trial. But they did appear as witnesses; *we* called them.

The second accusation, based on information leaked to *Life* by Morgenthau's staff, was that I had supposedly taken the Fifth Amendment before the grand jury. The truth is that I had never even testified before the particular Morgenthau grand jury that returned the indictment about to go on trial. They must have been referring to one of my countless appearances before what were known around the United States Court House as "Cohn Grand Juries One through Four." Aside from violating the law and civil and personal rights by leaking information about grand-jury proceedings, Morgenthau misinformed *Life* once again. They must have been referring to a detailed statement I made when being questioned by Perito, in which I outlined the incredible harassment I and my friends and associates have been put through, and concluded that I had had it insofar as "cooperating" with Morgenthau's attempts to get me.

Life had headed the last page of the article: "Joe McCarthy's boy takes the Fifth Amendment," but at the last minute, after the article was in print, it seems that *Life* and Morgenthau realized they had gone too far. They hastily attempted to change the headline to "Joe McCarthy's boy is still the champion of 'chutzpah.' " After spending thousands of dollars on reprints, they succeeded only partially in attempting to conceal their mistake—many editions bearing the original copy were circulated. This will be to our advantage in the libel suit.

I cannot regret the embarrassment my second acquittal must have brought to Lambert and *Life*. Reportedly, Lambert is still going around shaking his head in disbelief. Tom Bolan recently reminded me of a sentence in the article: "Thanks mainly to Cohn's noisy insistence that the attorney [Morgenthau] is persecuting him, the trial—whose issues will not be weighed here—shapes up as the critical confrontation of a long-run grudge match."

My acquittal might have been the "critical confrontation" in *Life*'s "long-run grudge match" as well.

X

Some Needed Reforms

Abolish the Grand-Jury System

COMING FROM A prosecutor of the Rosenbergs and the chief counsel for the McCarthy Committee, the suggestion that the grand-jury system be abolished might surprise many—some pleasantly, some otherwise. England abolished the grand-jury system in 1932. I think that on balance it has now outlived its usefulness in the United States.

What is a grand jury, and how does it function? A grand jury does not try people. It investigates and then makes a formal charge of commission of crime, which formal charge is called an indictment. A grand jury has twenty-three members, who are selected in generally the same way as trial jurors but who are supposedly more experienced and sophisticated.

To indict, the affirmative votes of twelve—a majority—are necessary. A grand jury sits in secret. The grand jurors and the prosecutors are sworn to secrecy, but we all know that this is honored in the breach ofttimes, as certain prosecutors leak out reports of developments before a grand jury.

In my case one could get a more accurate account of the "secret" grand-jury proceedings by reading James Wechsler's column in the New York *Post,* which was the most frequent vehicle for Morgenthau's "leaks" about me. The prosecutor acts as the counsel to the grand jury and customarily presents what cases he wishes to it and keeps away from it those he chooses to. Witnesses before the grand jury are not allowed to have counsel in the room with them while they are being questioned. In contrast to this, the McCarthy Committee invariably permitted witnesses to have counsel at their side in both secret and open session—and a congressional committee does not have the power to prefer criminal charges as does a grand jury. At one time the legal test for indictment was that a criminal charge could not be preferred unless the prosecutor made out a prima facie case before the grand jury —enough evidence which, if believed, would warrant a trial jury in convicting. But court decisions have watered down that standard to nothing, so that a grand jury can do as it pleases or, more accurately, as the prosecutor pleases it to do. With no meaningful quantum of evidence required and with a denial of rights to counsel being present, the use of a grand jury's name on top of an indictment seems to me to be a deception which lends unwarranted prestige to what is really a particular prosecutor's charge rather than a grand jury's.

Some judges lend almost ludicrously ritualistic support to the grand-jury fiction. The judge at my 1969 trial was horrified that I would suggest that Morgenthau was after me— it was up to the "grand jury." A perfect example of this whole fiction occurred at my first trial. The foreman of the grand jury that returned the indictment was called as a witness by the prosecutor to establish the materiality of questions on which perjury counts were based. Under cross-examination he didn't even know the names of conspirators alleged in the indictment or what witnesses had testified. It was quite apparent that the grand jury had just rubber-stamped Morgenthau.

Take the indictment: It is written by an assistant in Morgenthau's office. Most grand jurors don't have a remote idea as to what it says or why. In view of all these considerations why should a prosecutor be able to hide behind a grand jury's skirts for acts that are his, not theirs? Let a trial jury know the truth about where a charge emanates, and eliminate this legal fiction.

When I was a prosecutor, some of my most rewarding work was done with grand juries. I worked with them and tried to use them to perform a legitimate investigative function. I did not use them as rubber stamps for action that had been preordained by my superiors. In fact, one grand jury filed a presentment documenting heavy infiltration by American Communists in the United Nations over the specific objection of some of my superiors in the Justice Department. I supported the grand jury. But now it has vitually lost its dichotomous role as an investigative body and as a protector of the rights of potential defendants. It has been relegated into a back-seat position where most times, in effect, it rubber-stamps the prosecutor's wish and gives no protection to a potential defendant. The Supreme Court has also held that virtually no competent evidence need be presented to a grand jury before it can indict, thus making the system even more meaningless. Formal rules of evidence do not obtain before grand juries. But it had been thought that before a grand jury could vote an indictment, at least a minimum amount of competent and legally admissible evidence would have to be introduced. In other words, granting that hearsay and other types of evidence that would be excluded at a trial are allowed before a grand jury, it was assumed that in addition to the inadmissible evidence, there should be at least enough competent evidence to warrant the grand jury in finding a prima facie case and indicting. But the Supreme Court in the Costello case ruled otherwise, so that insofar as protecting a defendant, the grand jury might as well not be around.

Moreover, Morgenthau, for example (he is not alone), has

gelded grand juries to the point that he did not even permit jurors to ask questions directly of a witness or a potential defendant. In my day grand jurors were always permitted to ask questions of the witness. That is what they were there for. They were to investigate, ask questions, and determine whether there was enough to bring in an indictment and require the defendant to stand trial before a regular jury. Under these circumstances the system becomes an affirmative evil, because when a defendant is indicted by the grand jury and goes to trial, he is faced with the awesome burden of persuading a jury that they should in effect overrule what the grand jury did. Of course, a grand jury cannot "convict" anyone. It cannot find one guilty of a crime. It has heard no cross-examination of witnesses. Usually, it hears only witnesses produced by the prosecution and none by the defense. In fact, often the potential defendant does not even know that the grand-jury investigation is in progress. Therefore, all a grand jury can do is "indict," which means to prefer a charge, to accuse. It is like a plaintiff in a civil suit filing a complaint, which must then be answered by the defendant, and a trial takes place. If an indicted defendant in a criminal case pleads not guilty, he has thereby denied each and every charge in the indictment, and at a trial the prosecution must prove his guilt beyond a reasonable doubt. At a trial the judge must instruct the jury that they must regard the indictment as no evidence of guilt whatsoever but merely the formal way of instituting a criminal proceeding. This is, as one of our distinguished federal judges from the Third Circuit put it, one of those "ritualistic instructions to perform a psychologically impossible feat."

Curtail the Use of the Conspiracy Statute

A criminal conspiracy is an agreement between two or more persons to violate some criminal law. The conspiracy itself is a separate crime even if the law is actually violated. If two or more people agree to rob a bank, and then actually do it, they can be prosecuted for both the conspiracy to rob and the actual robbery, or either without the other. The decision as to whether or not to include a conspiracy count is a strictly tactical one made by the prosecutor. He usually decides to use it because of the advantages of getting in certain testimony against defendants that would otherwise be inadmissible and for other tactical reasons. The agreement itself is not enough to make out the crime of conspiracy but also requires that any one of the conspirators commit some "overt" act to carry the agreement out of the talking stage.

The overt-act requirement has become a joke—a telephone call, walking across the street, or entering someone's office are sufficient overt acts. In fact, I can't think of what, other than breathing, fails to qualify legally as an overt act. Here is a typical overt act from a recent conspiracy indictment, carrying a twenty-year prison sentence: "On or about November 9, 1968, the defendant . . . and co-conspirator . . . went to Jack Dempsey's restaurant, New York, New York."

The basic principle of punishing conspiracies to commit crimes might well be sound on the nipping-in-the-bud and deterrent theories. That is, if the accused are caught before they actually commit the crime, there is logic to punishing them for what amounts to an attempt, even though the execution itself fails. If robbers are apprehended outside a bank with guns and a diagram illustrating how they were going to break into the vault, they should be prosecuted for conspiracy. But if they are charged with having pulled off the actual robbery, what purpose is there in also charging them with a conspiracy to do what they did? The fact is that the conspiracy statute has been extended and expanded to such a degree by prosecutors and courts that actual substantive crimes like murder, rape, or treason don't seem anywhere near as pernicious as "conspiracy."

When there is a conspiracy count in an indictment, the

trial judge often receives evidence that would otherwise be promptly excluded as unreliable hearsay. The theory is this: If two or more persons are in a conspiracy, the law applies the principle of agency and holds that each one is acting for the others, so that what any one does is admissible against or binding upon the other conspirators even if they didn't say it, hear it, do it, or even think it. The only requirement is that it be in furtherance of the conspiracy.

For example, under a charge that I conspired with Weisman, Morton Weinberg, Patrusky, and six others to bribe Reicher, anything any of them did in this regard becomes binding on me, whether I knew about it or not. If Reicher testifies that Weisman told him, "Roy Cohn is in on this bribery," this is admissible against me, even though I was not present and that statement is untrue. Of course, if there were no conspiracy charge, what Weisman said to a third party about me out of my presence would not be admissible against me —it would be excluded as rank hearsay.

Further, certain judges love to charge the jury that conspiracy is much worse than an individual committing a crime, because the association of two or more makes it more effective and damaging to the public. To hear some judges deliver a charge on conspiracy, one would think it worse than selling a hundred kilos of heroin to grade-school children. Here is Judge Wyatt's charge to the jury in my case, and it plays funny games with logic:

> Now, let's think for a few minutes about conspiracy. A conspiracy, sometimes referred to as a partnership in crime, presents a greater potential threat to the public than the lone, single wrongdoer.
>
> Concerted action for criminal purposes generally makes it possible to accomplish more important and more complex results than those which an individual acting alone could accomplish.

Group association also increases the likelihood that the criminal venture will be successful. At the same time group association renders detection more difficult than where one individual is acting alone.

Perhaps the greatest evil of the conspiracy statute is a device known as naming certain persons as conspirators, but not as defendants. This is a favorite trick of certain prosecutors. If the "grand jury" indicts you, you are a defendant, and with innocence and a lot of luck you can be acquitted and exonerated. But the "grand jury" can also name other persons as conspirators, but not as defendants. This means that they were in the conspiracy, but the "grand jury" decides to list them as such without indicting them. The good, I suppose, is that they cannot go to jail. The evil for them is that they are smeared in the publicity on the indictment and have no opportunity to defend themselves. The evil for the defendants on trial is that by throwing in names of people as conspirators, their statements can perforce be used against the defendants.

The first fiction in this system is that the "grand jury" names the other conspirators. One does not even have to speculate that the grand jury doesn't even know the names it has supposedly listed as conspirators. All one needs is the surprising knowledge that after the indictment has been filed, and long after the grand jury has been discharged and has ceased to exist, the prosecutor, in filing a bill of particulars, can in effect amend the indictment and throw in the names of anyone he wishes as conspirators.

In my 1969 trial this is just what happened. The indictment was filed in January. In July Morgenthau listed six more people as conspirators who were not named as such in the indictment. My 1964 trial provides other examples of this abuse. Morgenthau listed as "conspirators" one of my law partners and the firm that did our accounting work. This was publicized. But there was not one iota of evidence against either at the trial. In fact, the accounting firm's name was not mentioned even once during the entire case of the prosecution. Obviously, they had been listed as conspirators only because Morgenthau's assistants were petulantly annoyed at them, believing they had not told all they knew about me.

Before the first trial Tom Bolan was in Judge Dawson's chambers at a pretrial discussion. Assistant prosecutor Gerald Walpin was present. Walpin had the depth of arrogance that is characteristic of little tyrants clothed with some temporary power. Perito, an assistant prosecutor of the 1969 trial, was his prototype with the same kind of empty pomposity. (I remember being rather dismayed one morning at the 1969 trial witnessing Perito, in his early thirties, grab a sixty-five-year-old marshal and order him to eject a seventy-year-old retired stenographer for the U.S. Attorney's office from a "reserved" row in the courtroom.) An exchange developed between Bolan and Walpin on the subject of who the prosecution contended were conspirators of mine one day shortly before my first trial in 1964. The setting was in Judge Dawson's chambers. Bolan asked if anyone was going to be added to the conspirators listed in the indictment. Walpin smirked and said he was thinking of adding one but was being lenient because the one of whom he was thinking was a member of the bar. There was a pregnant silence and Tom realized that Walpin was threatening to name Tom as a conspirator. Tom is not one to threaten. He said to Walpin: "Apparently, you mean me. Go right ahead and try it." Walpin retreated. Later, Tom commented: "You know, the little so-and-so could actually have done it—the looseness in this grand-jury conspiracy procedure might let him." And at the time of the conversation the grand jury had been out of existence for months.

Today's indiscriminate use of the conspiracy statute reminds me of false and misleading advertising to sell a usually defective product.

Another victim of overuse of the conspiracy statute is the

doctrine of law and order. Mass conspiracy trials are breeding grounds for violence and disorder. In this crop of cases arising from the peccadillos of the revolutionary New Left, a mass conspiracy trial affords them a stage on which to perform their weird play. Trying them individually for specific crimes when the facts warrant it would seem to make a lot more sense all around.

A good argument can be made for the retention of the conspiracy statute, but it would seem that its application should be restricted to those instances where the substantive crime is not committed and charged. And the open-sewer violation of carefully developed rules of evidence should no longer be countenanced. With good reason Judge Learned Hand described conspiracy as "the darling of the prosecutor's nursery."

Safeguards As to Accomplice Witnesses

In these days of widespread use of Valachi, Itkin, and Patrusky types, with actual injustice sometimes resulting and too many close calls for comfort, I believe we must shore up our legal standards for evaluating the testimony of accomplice witnesses. I suggest two ways:

1. The law of New York State does not permit conviction on the uncorroborated testimony of an accomplice. It requires corroborative evidence. I would extend this requirement to federal law, which as of now permits conviction on the uncorroborated word of an accomplice.

2. I would require that an accomplice who had pleaded guilty or had the prosecution against him severed and who is to testify as a prosecution witness against the other defendants be sentenced himself before he gives testimony.

In these two ways we have some insurance against injustice resulting from accomplice testimony.

The first way, already in effect in New York, does not hamper the administration of justice. Requiring some kind of corroboration at least gives us some outside, unconnected reason to believe that the accomplice witness is telling the truth, so that we are entirely dependent on the word of one whose moral character and lack of respect for law and truth are such that by his own admission he willingly participated in criminal activity. Legal history is replete with examples of accomplices who invented stories and involvement of others to say what was necessary to save their own necks.

Even more troublesome is the widespread practice of making a deal with an accomplice, by which he will get a suspended sentence or a light sentence for his confessed crime in return for testifying against his codefendants. Knowing the character of most accomplice witnesses, the prosecutor will not trust him by performing his end of the bargain— the break on sentence—until after the accomplice has testified, because if the accomplice is sentenced first, he is no longer in fear of the prosecutor and might not tell the story he's expected to at his codefendant's trial. So his sentence is "deferred" until after he has performed on the witness stand. Of course, implicit in this is an admission that the accomplice is not being truthful out of reform or remorse of conscience. Also implicit is that not even the prosecutor is willing to trust him, as he asks the jury to. Nevertheless, this "deferral" practice is widely used by prosecutors and condoned by many judges. Garfield, Roen, and Swann, for example, pleaded guilty in March, 1962. Customarily and logically, the time for sentencing is after the plea of guilty. These three were not sentenced after their pleas. They were not even sentenced after the conclusion of the United Dye trial at which they had pleaded guilty. Their sentences were "deferred" until after they had testified against me in the spring and summer of 1964, and it was only then—two years after their pleas of guilty—that Morgenthau delivered on his promise to them of suspended sentences.

A perfect example of this jockeying with justice comes

from my last trial. Muscat and Krock were indicted for false filings with Government agencies. They used the usual key to the jail door by making a deal with Morgenthau to testify against me in return for leniency for themselves—the same type of deal that Weisman admitted on the stand Morgenthau had made with him. Muscat and Krock therefore pleaded guilty in November, 1969. Their pleas of guilty were not made in the courtroom where such pleas are usually accepted but, through a special arrangement, were made before Judge Wyatt. Their sentences were then "deferred" until January and February, 1970. With this hanging over their heads they were ushered downstairs to testify against me. They did. And the jury disbelieved them and acquitted me. But there was another problem. There was still pending against me the old indictment, the merits of which I do not touch on here. Muscat and Krock were the principal witnesses Morgenthau had planned to use in that case before he dropped it in favor of the "Fifth Avenue" indictment. So the prosecution was still unwilling to perform for Muscat and Krock, as it might need them again. Their sentencing was constantly postponed from January, 1970, until June, 1970. By June, both the prosecution and the judge were running out of excuses for postponement. The following colloquy before Judge Wyatt on June 19, 1970, tells the story:

Referring to the old indictment, Judge Wyatt said, "And it is expected that Mr. Muscat and Mr. Krock will testify at that trial?" He continued: "And do I understand that Mr. Muscat and Mr. Krock through counsel want the Court at the time of sentencing to take into account the extent to which they cooperate with the Government and the extent to which they tell the truth as witnesses in this matter?" On receiving affirmative answers, Wyatt put the sentences off again, this time until December 4, 1970. Of course, on December 4, 1970, he slid them over to May 15, 1971. Now, since when is it justice for a judge to reward convicts for "cooperating" with the Government after a jury has found that their "cooperation" consisted of telling lies? Judge Wyatt presided at my trial. He knew that if the jury had believed Muscat and Krock, I would have been convicted.

The second part of Judge Wyatt's statement is even more outrageous. He says that on sentencing, the Court will consider "the extent to which they [Muscat and Krock] tell the truth as witnesses. . . ." But a jury has already determined that they did not tell the truth, and Judge Wyatt acknowledged in his charge that basic foundation of American jurisprudence that determination of the truth and issues of credibility are for a jury of one's peers, not for the judge. By what authority does Judge Wyatt propose to reach a conclusion opposite to that of the jury on an issue exclusively within their province? This judicial straining to provide a subterfuge for the obvious fact that the prosecution wanted to keep the constant threat of a jail sentence hanging over their heads in case they don't dance to the prosecution's tune was too much for even Muscat's and Krock's lawyers to swallow. They came up with another subterfuge—which I must say isn't too much more imaginative than Judge Wyatt's. They argued in effect that until another trial of me on related issues, nobody could be sure of the relative culpability of Muscat and Krock on charges to which they had already pleaded guilty. Incidentally, while Mr. Muscat, who was offered by the prosecution to the jury at my trial as a reformed, truthful person, has been at liberty due to deferral of his sentence, the Securities and Exchange Commission itself has charged in a formal complaint filed in federal court that in May, 1970, Mr. Muscat spent the free time he received as a result of Judge Wyatt's largess in deferring sentence by manipulating stock to phony up the amount of money he had agreed to pay in a business deal. And after these charges were made, Muscat did not dispute them but accepted a "consent" injunction.

Finally, this "deferral" practice might actually constitute a crime. Section 20(h) of Title 18 of the United States Code provides that it is a crime to give anything of value to "any person for or because of his testimony." Isn't freedom given by the prosecution something of value?

Let's bring treatment of accomplice witnesses up to at least the minimum standards that offer some assurance of truthfulness by requiring in federal law corroboration as it is required by New York State law and by having sentence imposed at the appropriate time so that a jury may accurately evaluate the motives of the witness.

Must Everything Be a "Federal Case"?

The term "federal case" has long been a colloquial synonym for "big deal." It is no longer a joke. If the present trend continues, everything from spitting on the sidewalk on up is in danger of becoming a federal crime.

Federal criminal power flows from the "implied powers" clause of the Constitution. It was meant to be exercised to enforce federal authority and to protect areas that were within federal jurisdiction. Borrowing a page from much of the New Deal legislation that, under the guise of the interstate commerce powers, made subject to federal laws a bricklayer on a building that had a tenant who mailed samples out of state, crass, attenuated reasoning is being attempted in criminal law.

Constitutionally, traditionally, and logically, violations of state and local laws have been enforced by state and local law-enforcement officials. But lately everything is becoming a "federal case." In my last "Federal case" District Attorney Hogan's office had determined that Reicher was the culprit and indicted him for grand larceny and perjury. He pleaded guilty to the indictment. Years later, Morgenthau decided he wanted to go after me again and to use Reicher as a Government witness, but he had to find a way to make a case that New York County had already declined to prosecute, a "federal case." This was attempted by having Reicher say I had given him money at the United States Court House, which is a "federal reservation," meaning that a state crime committed there can also be prosecuted federally. The rest of the fill-in came from the "travel act," meaning if anyone in the "conspiracy" travels or makes a long-distance call, what could only be a state crime is suddenly transformed into a federal case.

The whole DeSapio federal trial was pegged on con man Itkin's testimony that when he first met DeSapio at a party in upstate New York, Itkin traveled from New York City to northern New York by taking a bridge to New Jersey and then coming back into New York!

Late in 1970 Tom Bolan and I pored over a statute that seemed to make using threats to recover money you had loaned a federal crime! We could find no requirement in the statute of use of interstate facilities or of any federal angle. I asked a federal prosecutor I know if I had missed something. He replied: "Oh, no. Congress presumed that in some way or another people doing something like that must have contemplated doing something with an interstate angle to it." The constitutionality of this statute is now before the Supreme Court. We have able law-enforcement officials in states and localities throughout the nation. It was never contemplated that they be rendered ineffective and *functus officio* by a phony extension of federal power to cover everything including the kitchen sink, when there is no truthful or rational basis for such a fiction.

Conclusion

ONCE IN A while I give talks at law schools around the country. I realize that I am invited as something of a novelty because few people have had the variegated contacts with criminal law that I have had. I generally begin by saying: "My experience with the criminal law has been as a prosecutor, an investigator, counsel for a legislative committee, a teacher of law, an author of law review articles, often a witness, and almost as often a defendant."

At this point in my talks I acknowledge what many people have already guessed about me as a result of my background and my guilt by association—that I am a conservative.

As one who has gone through his own trials and tribulations, I am a firm believer in American justice. Before the jury came in at my first trial in July, 1964, I had written out a short statement I intended to issue in the event that the verdict had gone against me. I don't think I ever showed it to anyone. It went: "Despite this individual injustice to me, my faith in this country and its basic system of law remains today as strong as it ever was."

Not illogically, as a labeled conservative, I advocate renewed attention to the principle of law and order. The phrase "law and order" has become a hate word to adherents of the political left. Yet if we examine what I perceive as law and order, I might shock some of my friends in the liberal establishment, because they would realize that I share many of their views and concerns.

Concern for law and order is not a call to totalitarian rule and a declaration of martial law, as some would have us believe. Conservatives do *not* believe in that and never have. I believe in the protection of individual rights in criminal proceedings, and I have tried in this book to point out how certain shortcomings in our system create abuse.

My commitment to this respect for the Bill of Rights is not newly born as a result of my own recent experiences. For example, as counsel for the Senate Investigations Subcommittee, I almost invariably declined to initiate contempt proceedings against witnesses who asserted constitutional privileges.

The greatest threat to maintaining the protection of individual rights today arises not from conservatives, but from the actions during the past few years of the New Left. Their actions—ranging in degree from permissiveness to outright call for revolution—have so appalled the American public that a national reaction has set in against anything that can be construed as curtailing tough enforcement of law and order. Their planned behavior to induce riots throughout the country and cause general upheaval has lost them and their cause the silence of millions of middle-of-the-road Americans. And with this reaction there has come an impatience with the protection of individual rights.

Therein lies the irony. Many Americans are tired of bombings, campus takeovers, and the threat to their communities. The "silent majority" *demands* protection and sterner enforcement of laws. Conservatives have not caused this reaction. Responsibility falls foursquare on the irresponsible acts and conduct of the New Left.

My positions concerning protection of individual rights in criminal proceedings and the right to privacy against mail interception and indiscriminate bugging and wiretapping I consider to be conservative. I have lived through instances of these, and I challenge anyone else who has gone through abusive invasion of privacy to think otherwise.

In this book I have advocated certain reforms of our system of justice. I advocate them because justice and rights of the individual can be seriously jeopardized by the misuse of power by individuals who are placed in pivotal positions of law enforcement. But for every temporary holder of power like Morgenthau and Garrison there are hundreds of just and competent district attorneys across the country. Men like District Attorneys Frank Hogan in New York County and Burton Roberts in the Bronx epitomize the integrity of this office.

And for every instance of police brutality come hundreds of examples of heroism on the part of local police forces throughout the country. I am personally appalled at the abuse and name-calling that police have been forced to endure. These are the same police who have often given their lives protecting the rights of individuals in troubled communities and cities.

Next to the police, no law-enforcement agency has endured as much abuse by the New Left as the FBI. Since 1948, when I first entered the United States Attorney's office, I have watched the FBI in action. I have seen it fight Nazism and communism. I have seen it fight drug rings and kidnappers. Latterly, I have observed FBI agents who have appeared as adverse witnesses at trials in which I was defense counsel. Being advantaged by a view of its work from every standpoint, my regard for the integrity and dedication of the FBI and its director, J. Edgar Hoover, has increased. All too often the FBI doesn't get the credit it deserves for making our lives safer.

There is no dispute over the difficulty of the times in which we live. Threats to physical safety and fear of walking in the streets pervade our lives. Drug addiction and crimes connected with it have risen dramatically. Yet the New Left is so concerned with protecting the rights of the fringe elements of our society that protection of the community and appropriate action by local police forces is threatened. The New

Left believes that constitutional rights cover rioting and lawlessness. In effect their aim is to trample the rights of others while being fully protected by the law themselves. This is morally wrong and legally unsound. Certain members of the legal profession have been among the worst offenders. The answer to impatience with a miserable judge can never be to hurl objects or epithets in a courtroom. A sound defense at criminal trials was never supplemented by pickets or riots.

I don't buy this type of conduct. By the same token I don't buy the view of certain commentators who share my "law and order" views but maintain that safeguards of individual rights and observance of certain technical legal procedures totally hamper law-enforcement officials. I think this is more fancied than real. The hampering seems due less to the law than to political interference on a policy level by certain big-city officials who think they hold their franchise for the benefit of the local hippie community and black-power pressure groups, rather than for the protection of the people as a whole.

Where does it all lead? It leads to this: I have been on trial myself and have seen the process of justice go awry because it was placed in dangerous hands. I have defended others who have been on trial and have done everything possible to insure their rights. On the one hand, I don't want to tie the hands of police and law-enforcement agencies trying to do their jobs to protect the public. On the other hand, I don't want to deprive any individual of his right to a fair trial and due process of justice. I regard these positions as compatible.

I do not recommend as therapy the legal ordeals I have undergone. But I emerge from them firm in the belief that solutions to the ills that beset our society can be found within the framework of our own system of justice, and firm in the belief that our system of justice is, like our country, the finest in the world.

INDEX

Index

192   A FOOL FOR A CLIENT

United Dye case (cont.)
  Gillespie, S. Hazard, testimony, 22
  grand-jury investigation, 18
  presiding judge at, 62–63
  Robson, Morton S., incident, 19–20, 21, 22, 23
United Nations, 104, 166
United States Agency for International Development (AID), 66
United States Code, 176
United States Justice Department, 134, 166
  Criminal Tax Division, 130
United States Supreme Court, 5, 139, 166, 177
United States Treasury Department, 8–9

Valachi, Joe, 45–46
Van Allen, John, 15
Vassallo, John, 136
Vogue (magazine), 99

Wagner, Richard, 27, 30
Wall Street Journal, 106, 115
Walpin, Gerald, 16, 121, 122, 123, 124, 149, 171
Walters, Barbara, 131–132

Wechsler, James, 140, 165
Weinberg, Harry, 27–28, 29, 30, 31, 32, 38, 39
Weinberg, Morton, 2, 28, 32, 35, 41, 45, 141, 169
Weinfeld, Edward, 63
Weinstein, Herbie, 54–55, 56, 57, 58, 71, 96, 97–98, 126
Weisman, Lawrence I., 26, 28, 31–41, 45, 51, 63, 71, 72, 74, 81, 91, 100, 101, 103, 104, 107, 116, 141, 158–159, 169
Weisman, William, 35
Welch, Joseph, 83
Wheeler, Keith, 42
White, Harry Dexter, 8
Williams, Paul, 121
Wiretapping, 139–140
Wyatt, Inzer B., 52–53, 56, 58, 65–82, 87, 88, 89, 91, 92, 99, 106, 109–110, 124, 155, 169–170, 174–175

Yonkers *Herald Statesman,* 123

Zion, Sidney, 138